Navigating the Course

A Man's Place in His Time

by

David Fanshel

Valley Meadow Press
2010

Navigating the Course: A Man's Place in His Time

Copyright © 2010 David Fanshel
All rights reserved

Orders for additional copies of *Navigating the Course* may be obtained by writing:
    David Fanshel
    c/o The Redwoods
    40 Camino Alto
    Mill Valley, CA 94941

Photos pages 20, 24, and 88 courtesy of Milstein Division of United States History, Local History & Genealogy, The New York Public Library, Astor, Lenox and Tilden Foundations.

Photo page 54 courtesy of photography collections, Miriam and Ira D. Wallach Division of Art, Prints and Photographs, The New York Public Library, Astor, Lenox and Tilden Foundations.

Photos pages 140 and 202 courtesy of 450th bombardment group website, www.450thbg.com.

"The Vortex of History" appears on 450th bombardment group website, www.450thbg.com.

Printed in the United States of America.

Valley Meadow Press
ISBN: 978-0-972369-6-4

Navigating the Course

A Man's Place in His Time

The Fanshel Family circa 1928

This book is dedicated to my wife Florence (Greenberg) Fanshel. Over the 52 years of our marriage, she encouraged my writing with generosity of spirit. She was always enthusiastically ready to read back the results of my written labors. She remains at my side in memory.

Contents

Introduction		11
Part One: Childhood in the Bronx		
1	Bargaining as Sport	17
2	David, the Bar Mitzvah Boy	25
3	Fanshel Family History	35
4	Hyman Fanshel	47
5	Thanksgiving in the Bronx, 1936	55
6	The Firstborn Son Returns	67
7	Caught in the Squeeze	77
8	Life Resumes	91
Part Two: Participating in WWII		
9	Into the Wild Blue Yonder	103
10	Crossing the Atlantic	125
11	A Chilly Reception for Replacement Crews	141
12	In the Vortex of History	159

13	Clearing Myself with God	169
14	The Chief Currency of Life	179
15	Last Days of the Budapest Clunker	189
16	The Fickle Finger of Fate	203
17	Goodby, Manduria	213
18	Christmas in Casablanca	221
19	Two Flyboys Home from the Air War	233
20	Epilogue: The Ultimate Absurdity	241
Acknowledgements		249
Published Books by David Fanshel		251
About the Author		253

List of Illustrations

Fanshel Family, circa 1928	frontispiece
The Four Fanshel Siblings, circa 1931	16
A Market Scene on Orchard Street, 1937	20
The Jacob H. Schiff Center	24
Uncle Sam and Aunt Dora Kratchman	32
Clara and Hyman Fanshel, Odessa, Russia, 1910	34
Clara Kratchman as a Young Woman	37
The Fanshel Family in Russia	39
Aunt Bluma and Uncle Morris Winitt	42
Aunt Sonia Kratchman [Kaplan] and Uncle Irving Kratchman	44
A Group of Zionist Youth to which Hyman Belonged	46
The West Washington Market, Manhatten, 1936	54
The Fanshel Family, circa 1931	66
The Author's Brother Jack Fanshel	76
Poe Park	88

Hyman and Clara Fanshel	90
Uncle Irving, Owner of the Fair Deal Dairy	96
Dave Fanshel, High School Yearbook Photo, 1941	102
Clara and Hyman Fanshel Visit David in Atlantic City	109
Dave Fanshel, "Flyboy"	114
The *Myakin'* Crew at Biggs Field, El Paso, Texas, May 1944	124
Myakin' in Flight	140
Plaque: "In Honor of Those Who Served with the 450th"	157
Lobau, Austria, Oil Storage Facility Bomb Strike Photo, August 22, 1944	158
Flying Officers of B-24 *Myakin'*	168
A B-24 Dropping Payload	178
German Anti-aircraft Flak Viewed from a Plane	183
Budapest Bomb Strike Photo	188
Toulon Submarine Pen Bomb Strike Photo	193
Myakin' Flying in Formation	202
Dave Fanshel at the End of His Tour of Combat Duty	212
Pilot Jim McLain and the B-24 Liberator *Myakin'*	220
The Author with His Sister, Ruth, January 1945	232
Ferrara Railroad Bridge Bomb Strike Photo	240

Introduction

Born in the Bronx, New York, in 1923, I grew up knowing that the land of Russia had significant meaning for the Fanshel family. The country of the czars was a great source of Jewish immigration to the United States after World War I. Generations back, the Fanshels and their counterparts on the maternal side, the Kratchmans, lived in the small towns of Zabukridge and Krijopol, comical-sounding names to an American kid. These places were near Odessa, the major Black Sea port where Jews had established a significant historical presence. Years after my parents came to the United States, my father's brother and sister, Levi and Geitel, remained in the vicinity of Odessa.

The family had broken up in 1919, after the Bolshevik revolution. Chaotic social circumstances impelled my parents Hyman and Clara to flee westward through Europe with members of the Kratchman family. Geitel, a thirteen-year-old orphan, had to be left behind—despite her protests—in the care of Levi and his wife. The departing group, including my parents, their two young children, a maternal uncle, and two aunts, spent a year wandering in Belgium and France. Their nomadic status ended when my mother's brother, Irving Kratchman, and his business partner, Sidney Kaplan, joint owners of a food market in New York City, sent travel money to enable this assortment of Fanshels and

Kratchmans to come to America. As the lowest-paying passengers on an old ship, they endured harsh, unsanitary conditions in tight quarters. In this departure for a better life in a new country, my parents experienced the death of their younger child, a two-year-old girl, who became ill with diphtheria in the midst of the voyage. The pain created by their loss was so profound that my parents could never talk about the experience with us.

On their arrival in New York, more tribulations continued to dog the traveling family. Five-year-old Sol, my parents' surviving child, was stricken with scarlet fever. Federal immigration policies dictated that adults and children with serious contagious diseases be detained for deportation. When he was found to be ill by the immigration authorities, my brother was placed in an isolation ward in the detention hospital on Ellis Island. You can imagine the intense fear experienced by this young boy who had lost his little sister and was separated from his parents in strange surroundings where he did not understand the language. The family was in acute crisis.

Again, my Uncle Irving and his business partner, Sidney (later to become my uncle through marriage to my Aunt Sonia), came to the rescue. They spirited Sol out of a hospital window in the middle of the night, a transfer accomplished by bribing a guard with fifty dollars. While circumstances motivated this stratagem, I grew up feeling that breaking the law was not a high-toned way for a family to start life in America. In my child's view, the story of our entry pretty much placed us at the bottom of the heap. It seemed we were essentially outsiders, elbowing our way into the country.

Over time, a part of me came to redefine our immigration story with less disparagement of my origins. I felt grateful that my uncles had taken risks to make it possible for me to have a big brother eight years older than I. More effective than my parents as a teacher, Sol became the one who interpreted America for his three younger siblings. I came to realize that while we carried no prestigious name on a family coat of arms, what we did retain in our history was a reservoir of energy that supported our survival, leaving identifiable traits as if they were imprinted upon our genetic code: strong personality markers that could be easily identified even into the third generation. Stubbornness? In good measure. Passion? Yes, indeed, both in loving and hating.

Looking back from the vantage point of my later years, I could see to a greater extent the ways in which the family's beginnings and subsequent life in America influenced my understanding of the world and the individual I became. When I came to write about growing up in a Jewish immigrant family during the Depression, the narratives and memories were of family dynamics played out against the themes of poverty, cultural assimilation, and intergenerational conflict. In this regard, perhaps they are reminiscent of other portrayals of the struggles of ethnic families, for example, *Angela's Ashes* and *A Raisin in the Sun*.

In similar fashion, I have come to understand my combat experience in World War II as a B-24 crew-member as a significant milestone in my development. Much of this had to do with my being taken out of the cocoon-like environment of Jewish life in New York and being able, by my military experience, to share social intimacy with men of very different backgrounds. These differences, I realized, accounted for the fact many of the issues I confronted during the war, as described in this volume, did not exist for my crewmates and others I encountered in my military career. I consider myself fortunate to have had the benefit of these relationships and the opportunity to expand my view of the world and my place within the human stream.

Part One: Childhood in the Bronx

The Four Fanshel Siblings: Ruth, David, Jack, and Sol, circa 1931

1

Bargaining as Sport

My mother informed me one day of her decision to take me with her on one of her periodic shopping excursions to the Lower East Side of Manhattan. In addition to the purchase of various household items, she would expand her mission to include the purchase of a pair of pants for me.

As a twelve-year-old living in the midst of the Depression (it was 1935), I was elated; the experience of receiving a new item of clothing was relatively rare in our financially strapped family. I usually wore hand-me-downs from my older brother, Jack. Additionally, I welcomed the prospect of a break in my daily routine and an escape from the confines of our neighborhood. Our family resided in the northern part of the Bronx near the Grand Concourse in a pleasant-looking red brick six-story apartment house. Conditions in our two-bedroom apartment, however, were overcrowded for the six of us. My parents slept in one bedroom, and we three boys in the other, with Jack, fifteen, and me sharing one bed, and Sol, twenty years old, enjoying one for himself. My eight-year-old sister, Ruth, slept on the couch in the living room, and her bed was made up on a daily basis.

Given our modest means, my mother took pride in her housekeeping skills. She cared about appearances and used her creativity on projects that would make our apartment look stylish. Being an efficient homemaker was fundamental to her self-concept as a responsible manager of her home.

On this excursion, Mom planned to search for inexpensive fabrics at a remnants store for use in making slipcovers for the living room furniture. She was adept in the use of an old foot-pedaled Singer sewing machine, a versatile tool for many of her domestic projects. Her determined display of energy as she pumped the pedals left me in awe of her skill and dedication. Mom would also be on the lookout for materials she could use to make a party dress for Ruth.

Going shopping with my mother may seem mundane, but I was excited because it was a rare occasion to share personal time with her. Given that I was born eighteen months after my brother Jack, and with Ruth coming upon the scene four years after me, our living circumstances provided few opportunities for my mother and me to be together in our small apartment. The demands placed upon her time did not support much relaxed and affectionate interaction with her children. I have come to believe that I missed out on something important in my development because of this.

Mom often commented that I was born a *shtiller kind mit getokte* features ("a quiet child with fine" features). She was wont to say: "When I looked at him sleeping so peacefully, I decided to keep him." I must have had strong instincts for survival, since I often took the stance of the quiet observer. Under stressful family circumstances, my giving forth with a neonatal yell would surely have led to my extinction!

I tended to compensate for this family pattern of benign neglect by retreating into myself. This likely pushed me into reliance on an inner life, which permitted me to entertain myself, often in a dreamy sort of way. My withdrawal was sometimes noticed by my father, who did not quite understand my remoteness. He sometimes referred to me as a *stadrayter philosophe* ("a mixed-up philosopher").

Mom and I proceeded downtown by subway, about a forty-five-minute ride. We began our visit with the area around Union Square, where we could explore stores on Fourteenth Street, an important east-west commercial thoroughfare in downtown Manhattan. My mother appeared nervous when we entered the crowd of human bodies and cars swirling around us. I was abruptly pulled forward when Mom decided to cross the street, only to be yanked back to the sidewalk when she changed her mind. It was as if she remained the farm girl trying to cope with the big city of Odessa. Her uncertainty startled me, because she usually moved with ease in our Bronx neighborhood, even negotiating the clamor of the Grand Concourse.

We made our way to Orchard Street, a favorite place for bargain hunters. As we walked past the stores, I gazed at the multitude of colorful pushcarts lined up in the gutter displaying all kinds of wares for sale. I noticed retail stores specializing in the sale of Jewish prayer shawls, Bibles, and other religious objects. I was particularly taken, however, with the food stores, where whiffs of familiar foods made me hungry. One establishment advertised hot knishes, potato- or kasha-filled, a favorite food of the Fanshels, while another offered appetizing items such as sour pickles, herring, and sturgeon.

When we had gone a few more blocks, Mom spotted a retail store with a wooden sign offering the promotional message: "Isaac Sologonick—We Sell Pants to Last!"

The store must have impressed Mom as a likely place to begin her search for bargains, as she marched inside with me in tow. Because it was still early in the day, we were the only customers present. The surroundings appeared quite untidy, with many brands of trousers in high stacks distributed in a helter-skelter manner. The quantity of goods on display seemed greater than could be accommodated by the limited space available.

Mr. Sologonick sat drinking tea at a little desk cluttered with assorted papers. He seemed absorbed in reading his newspaper, which I recognized as the *Jewish Daily Forward*, though it rarely appeared in our household because my parents preferred *Der*

A Market Scene on Orchard Street, 1937 (Photo by Alexander Alland, Milstein Division of United States History, Local History & Genealogy, The New York Public Library, Astor, Lenox and Tilden Foundations)

Tag ("The Day"), a publication whose political stance they found more appealing. With a head of graying hair, a twisted black moustache, and horn-rim spectacles hanging precariously on a somewhat misshapen nose, perhaps broken in some accident, he appeared a bit older than Mom.

Speaking Yiddish, Mr. Sologonick introduced himself in a courtly manner. He informed us that he had been in business on this spot for almost twenty years, and expressed pride that he had customers coming from all over the city. When Mom informed him that she was looking for a pair of pants for her son, he nodded his head, but postponed talking about clothing. Instead, he asked, "Tell me, Missus—what is your name?

Sounds to me like you come from Minsk?" My mother took this expression of interest in her as a ploy to soften her up for a sale. She would have none of this nonsense, and her reply was brusque: "My name is Fanshel and I don't come from Minsk. I come from Odessa!"

Unruffled by Mom's display of irritation, her would-be interlocutor shrugged his shoulders and remarked that Minsk and Odessa were *both* in the Ukraine. "No big deal."

Annoyed by his continuing prattle, Mom let him have it straight. "Listen, Sologonick, I did not come here to have conversation with you about the old country. Tell me: Do you have a nice pair of pants for my David?"

Trying not to appear offended, Mr. Sologonick laughed uncertainly and waved his arms about. "You see that I have many nice pants." He began picking them up from several places and presenting them to my mother for consideration. "In this pile is the least expensive, and as you move to the right you'll get to some of my more special things. Look around and pick what catches your fancy. David can try the pants on behind the curtain in the back. Make sure the boy gets a good fit."

Despite his courtesy, I worried that Mr. Sologonick might feel challenged by my mother's feistiness. Steadfast in her purpose, she was clearly able to *handl* ("bargain"). However, since no other customers were present this morning, perhaps he did not mind having a chance to engage in such sport with her.

After rummaging through a selection of trousers, which she summarily rejected, Mom finally chose a pair made of gray herringbone tweed; they looked dressy and seemed well constructed. She inquired about the price, but when the information was given, she offered no reaction.

"Ah, Mrs. Fonchelle!" the proprietor exclaimed. "You know the *real* stuff when you see it. Handsome garment. And made of iron. Will last him until he gets married."

Mom stared at him with a blank face, not showing a flicker of a positive response. Her expression communicated clearly that he had failed to earn her respect and lacked any status as a person who could influence her.

As I tried on the pants, I was relieved that Mr. Sologonick and Mom were not going to have a wrestling match about the price. I was hopeful that I might actually get a pair of pants that suited my mother.

Looking at myself in the mirror, I perceived a flattering image. These trousers were a great improvement over the patched-up pants I always inherited from Jack. It would feel stylish to be dressed like a sport among my friends and classmates.

But my fantasies proved short-lived, and my self-indulgence evaporated abruptly when my mother suddenly made a surprise maneuver and confronted Mr. Sologonick with a demand for a major slashing of his previously quoted price. Her supreme self-confidence was impressive, but her behavior embarrassed me. To my mind, she was going way beyond the rules of acceptable behavior.

Mr. Sologonick suddenly realized that he was dealing with a skilled person who had learned to *handl* in America. Mom had neatly deflected his effort to win her over. After a pause, he tried to ingratiate himself by entering into negotiations with her in his most enticing manner, but his self-confidence faltered when he saw the look of utter disdain on Mom's face.

Mr. Sologonick's loss of nerve was made apparent by the eruption of considerable sweat on his forehead; especially revealing was his Adam's apple throbbing up and down under his chin like a yo-yo. In his frustration, Mr. Sologonick abandoned his position as a skilled player in this contest and allowed himself to get angry. Talking through clenched teeth, and peering intensely at my mother through narrowed eyes, he replied: "Mrs. Fonchelle, the last price I quoted is *final.* I run a business here, not a charity. The asking price is close to what I myself paid for the pants." With this retort, he turned his back to her. Mom engaged in a counterthrust. Cool as a cat, she scornfully tossed the pants onto the pile of her previous rejects. She grasped my arm and, with a military-style command, gave her orders: "Let's go! Enough of this henky-penky." At first, Mr. Sologonick looked furious, but he then tried to feign indifference. Without looking at my mother, he busied himself rearranging the assortment of discarded pants.

In my frustration, I had an enormous urge to tell my mother how *ridiculous* I thought all of this negotiating had been—*over a pair of pants*! But I could see there was no dissuading her from her decision.

In a state of total consternation, I found myself being dragged abruptly out of the store. I had no option but to follow Mom's lead as we marched up Orchard Street in the direction of the subway. I could see that all this *handlin* had come to naught. Thoroughly demoralized, I realized that I had gone on this trip to engage in a silly exercise. I struggled to hold back tears.

We had not gone very far when I heard a shrill voice coming from behind us. "Mrs. Fonchelle. Mrs. Fonchelle. Hold your horses!"

We stopped and turned around. It was Mr. Sologonick chasing after us, breathless, and with a look of desperation. His hands were thrust skywards as if in a pleading gesture to God, as he said to us: "Why are you running away? Reasonable people can talk things through. Come back and I'll make you an offer you can't refuse." I wondered, *What was going on?* But when I observed the emerging curl of a smile on Mom's face, it became clear to me that she realized that she had won.

We returned to the store. Mom bought the pants. And I rode home deliriously happy.

The Jacob H. Schiff Center (Milstein Division of United States History, Local History & Genealogy, The New York Public Library, Astor, Lenox and Tilden Foundations)

2

David, the Bar Mitzvah Boy

It was the summer of 1936, and my thirteenth birthday was coming up in a week. My father casually told me that he had arranged for my bar mitzvah, a religious service inducting me into the special status of a Jewish person. The event would take place in a few days at the Jacob H. Schiff Center, a few blocks from our home.

Housing one of the larger synagogues in the Bronx, the multi-purpose Schiff Center offered a variety of religious, educational, and recreational programs to the Jewish residents of the area. Except for my oldest brother, Sol, who was finishing his last year at City College of New York, we Fanshel kids attended the Center's after-school Hebrew classes, engaged in sports in the large gymnasium, and cavorted in the competition-sized swimming pool.

Outside of public school, I spent most of my time away from home at the Schiff Center— except, of course, during summer vacation, when my friends and I hung out in nearby Poc Park, a popular recreational area stretching two blocks on the Grand Concourse, the area's posh boulevard. Edgar Allen Poe's cottage, where he had lived for several years, was enshrined at the center of the park.

My father's way of organizing my bar mitzvah celebration was characteristically devoid of fancy trimmings. I would participate in the religious initiation ceremony on a Thursday morning when a *minyan*, that is, a quorum of congregation members, gathered to say morning prayers. A party would be held at our home on the following Sunday, with my mother taking responsibility for the shopping and cooking chores.

Providing me with a confirmation suit was another challenge that would energize my mother. When confronted with a child's need for an outfit, she had a predilection for making do with what was available, creating something serviceable without spending any money. It seemed that a piece of clothing never died in our family. A well-worn garment might be handed down from one child to the next, repaired on more than one occasion—often patched together in multicolored, sometimes mismatched, fabrics—and finally passed on to a relative or friend.

To insure my being properly fitted for this special milestone in my life, my mother, Clara, would employ her widely admired tailoring skills on the antiquated foot-pedaled Singer sewing machine. The blue serge suit to be altered would be going through its third iteration after being previously worn by Jack at his bar mitzvah two years before, and by my brother Sol six years before that. By now, there was a polishing effect visible on the seat of the trousers, and the garment glistened brightly in the sunshine.

Having my rite of passage take place on a Thursday morning in a small chapel and not in the resplendent main synagogue on Saturday was unusual in our middle-class neighborhood. While carrying out the bar mitzvah in this way was permitted by the religious practices of Judaism, resorting to such cost-cutting defined me socially as marginal compared to my contemporaries. Obviously, the Fanshels could not engage in the display of material affluence commonly mustered by other families for their bar mitzvah boys. Yet I was not surprised or especially burdened by this knowledge, because it fit with the way we lived. A lack of income had always been our family's main survival issue. Given our tight economic circumstances, we simply could not afford Schiff Center's charges for the Saturday service. Who had the money to pay the standard house fee for this occasion and also tender complimentary payments to the rabbi and the cantor?

Despite being invested in asserting his Jewishness *(Yiddishkeit)*, my father defined his obligations toward his God in his own inimitable way. In a variety of circumstances, he often expressed philosophical and pragmatic views about the democratic values that he felt should serve as the foundation for Judaism. In this, he held on to some of the socialist ideals intermixed with Zionism he espoused in his youth in Russia.

In regard to my father's orientation to religious ceremonial requirements, still fresh in my mind is an occasion in which he took me with him to a funeral parlor following the death of a family member. Hyman was often asked to undertake this difficult assignment because this was something he could manage sensibly. He was known within a large circle of family and friends as having the capacity for keeping his emotional equilibrium in the midst of the grieving and emotional chaos that surrounded the death of a loved one.

As we traveled there, I pondered why he had chosen me to accompany him. I asked myself: *"What does a young boy need to know about funeral arrangements? Perhaps Pop thinks I can someday be called upon to perform the same function on his behalf?"*

The funeral parlor staff person, sounding like a salesman, sought to impress upon Hyman the selling point that the deceased warranted a "tasteful" coffin as a reflection of the family's affection. My father tartly replied that his relative was not in a position to have any "taste" about the matter. He knew when he was alive that he belonged to us and that his family would not disown him or show anything but respect for the life he'd lived in our midst. In keeping with the tradition established in biblical times, my father dealt with the matter in no uncertain terms. "The cheapest pine box is all that is required to show respect for the dead." While I was embarrassed by a discourse that suggested financial haggling, which struck me as inappropriate on such a somber occasion, I later came to respect my father's obvious sense of his own self-worth and his desire to be in charge of his own ethical standards. He refused to be a pushover for people who tried to impose religious and social obligations on him to further their business interests, and he was determined not to shell out money to placate them.

The same hard-headed approach was employed when Hyman negotiated our going to Hebrew School at Schiff Center. He pressed to make the admissions person feel guilty about even asking for fees. My father's arguments were so compelling that, by the time he was through with the twists and turns of his dialectic, having to do with the Jewish community's obligation to educate its children, he had the woman's eyes bulging from their sockets. Thus it was agreed that our family would pay the paltry sum of a dollar a month tuition for each of us three children.

There was also the matter of our attendance at the synagogue at Schiff Center on the High Holy Days of Rosh Hashanah and Yom Kippur. It was standard procedure for reserved seats to be purchased for participation in the holy prayers, and the sale of tickets provided a major source of income to maintain the religious institution. Since the tickets were expensive, my father decided that, given our family's limited finances, we would sit in the less-expensive spillover facility, the gymnasium—no conservatory-trained cantor here—where we would have two of the folding chairs reserved for us. But there were four Fanshels who were supposed to attend: my father, my siblings Jack and Ruth, and myself. How was this to be handled? Simple. My father used the two tickets to go in with Jack, then Jack came out with the two tickets and got Ruth, and came out again to get me.

Early on the Thursday morning during the week of my birthday, I accompanied my father to the Schiff Center. The rest of the family was at home, my siblings getting ready to go to school and my mother busy performing her household chores. The message was clear: No alteration of normal routines was required.

My father and I entered a moderately large assembly room that could accommodate about two hundred people. It served as the chapel for daily morning prayers and was the meeting hall where students of the Hebrew School attended sabbath services. Aside from the cabinet in which the Torah was stored, there was no artistic adornment on the walls, and the setting was musty, almost depressing, in its threadbare quality. There was no rabbi or cantor present.

As we waited, twelve old men appeared and readied themselves for morning prayers. They looked a bit weary as they opened their velvet bags (*tefillin* in Yiddish) containing their prayer shawls. I was interested to observe this religious practice that Jewish men perform in the morning. They removed two small leather boxes containing biblical verses, which they fastened with leather straps to their foreheads and left arms, thereby meeting the obligation to bind the religious commandments to them.

Two young men had also come to pray before going to work. My father explained that they were meeting an obligation to attend prayer services for a year in accordance with established Jewish mourning practices. The time they invested in this activity was required as a mark of respect for their departed parents.

As the older participants had done, the young men opened pouches containing their *tefillin*. I remembered that my father had informed me several days earlier that he expected me to *"lay tvillen"* after my bar mitzvah. To my relief, I never took on this prayer obligation, because my father left for work every day at 4 A.M. and could not supervise me.

In short order, the congregants started their prayers in a monotone at a surprising breakneck speed. My father joined in, and it was soon clear to me that he knew the prayer book by heart and could outrace the others. I had an irreverent impulse to cheer my father on. *"Go to it, Pop, we can beat them!"*

Then attention turned to me, and I was called on to read from the day's passage in the Torah, which I had been prepared for by my father. He stood at my side as I struggled through the text in the traditional sing-song manner. He held his own with the other men when procedural issues arose, and I had a glimpse of my father's childhood as never before. I could more fully understand that his younger years must have been totally immersed in the liturgy of Judaism. I sensed that his parents and the religious life with which they surrounded him would probably seem exotic to me if I found myself among them. Yet, in his current situation living in America, economic necessity required him to work on Saturdays, and he was living in a more secular fashion than religious devotion would otherwise require of him.

Wearing my new *tallis* (prayer shawl) helped me feel special. An elderly white-bearded man with a huge *tallis* over his shoulders stroked my back gently as I recited the prayers. He murmured encouraging words in Yiddish as he swayed back and forth. Despite the nondescript nature of the occasion, I sensed warmth directed toward me from the older participants, and I gained some emotional lift from the experience.

When the service was over, my father introduced some conviviality by opening a bag with a bottle of Canadian Club whiskey, some cut-up herring, and a honey cake my mother had baked. Everyone helped themselves, and they drank a toast to me. *To life and devotion to the Torah! Lechaim! ("to life")*.

The following Sunday, about fifty people squeezed into our small two-bedroom apartment to celebrate my bar mitzvah. Uncles, aunts, cousins, *lansleiter* (fellow countrymen), and other friends were well represented. My mother had been cooking day and night for a week, and the prepared food had been stored in the refrigerators of neighbors scattered around us in our Bronx apartment house. My father's cousin Louis Feinstein was a small wholesaler in delicatessen products, and he amply supplied us with salami, corned beef, pastrami, and tongue. As a fruit merchant, my father had loaded our fire escape with several watermelons and boxes of cantaloupes, honeydew melons, strawberries, and cherries.

My mother had made large pots of stuffed cabbage and borscht and marinated meats. She had also baked strudel, nut cakes, and many kinds of cookies as accompaniments to the cooked fruit (compote) and tea.

Hyman provided a generous supply of wine made with his own hands from grapes obtained at Washington Market, the wholesale breadbasket of New York City. Bottles were stored throughout the apartment under beds and wherever space could be found. He had the reputation of being a sophisticated amateur vintner, and I can recall somewhat riotous family gatherings where we would sit around the kitchen table eating alcohol-soaked cherries left over from the preparation of *Wishnic* (a liqueur), which was his specialty. I remember leaving the table and staggering to my bed.

Almost all of the men present at my party owned small retail stores. They worked long hours, six days a week, and they sometimes helped out a relative or friend on a Sunday. They were in a constant state of exhaustion, and I sadly learned in later years that they would likely die of heart disease many years before their wives. For them, a party was a rare break from their stressful work lives, and they obviously relished the time they could spend together with others who shared their backgrounds.

My uncles and older cousins imbibed my father's wine with gusto. The interaction of alcohol and their chronic state of fatigue caused almost all of them to withdraw from participating in the party. Taking turns distributing themselves on beds in twos and threes, they snored away in deep naps, sounding like a symphony orchestra tuning up.

The women manifested a strong sense of rapport with each other. I was touched by the solicitude they demonstrated toward my mother, who had somehow managed this Herculean feat of feeding such a crowd by her own determination and her cooking and baking skills. Their affection for her flowed in an easy and natural manner, reflecting the fact that for many she had served as a benign second mother. The women had brought their own favorite dishes from home, and they worked diligently, serving, clearing tables, washing cooking utensils and dishes, making tea, and somehow controlling the children who seemed enlivened by the crowded conditions and the din.

Uncle Sam and Aunt Dora Kratchman. They came to America on the same boat with the author's parents shortly after being married in Russia. Their appearance, that of a handsome, modern couple, helped them to easily fit in with the American scene.

We were not a family where the children were indulged with presents. We kids did not expect such offerings, and when they were tendered we were surprised. A new shirt or tie was more likely given than a toy or a baseball. But a bar mitzvah sometimes evoked a special response. Ben Winitt, fifteen years older than me, and more like a brother than a cousin, and his wife, Ann, provided me with an expensive-looking chemistry set packaged in a shiny inlaid wooden box. Being a recipient of a such a gift was a novelty for me, and I cherished it for years as a symbol of their affection.

We Fanshel children and our Kratchman cousins constituted about a dozen emerging members of our extended families. We understood that as the next generation we were strongly connected to each other by our history. Aunt Sonia, Aunt Dora, and Uncle Sam had come with my parents on the boat to America; Uncle Irving and Uncle Sidney helped pay for the boat tickets; and Aunt Bluma and Uncle Morris provided sleeping arrangements during the first days ashore. Our togetherness was unshakable.

Organizing ourselves into age categories, we kids amused ourselves by going outdoors and playing games in the front of the house. Stickball, "immies" (marble shooting), rope jumping, and Johnnie-on-the-pony were just some of the games we played that showed we had joined the American stream.

That my bar mitzvah brought us together made me feel important.

Clara and Hyman Fanshel, Odessa, Russia, 1910

3

Fanshel Family History

Arriving in America from Russia in 1920, my parents settled in New York City, as did my mother's four siblings—two brothers and two sisters. The men were employed in running dairy stores and small laundries. Sharing the same immigration experiences, they were very close to one another. My father felt disadvantaged because his brother and sister had remained in Russia. To compensate for the unavailability of his siblings, he valued the ties he was able to maintain with cousins living in New York City, who had also come from Russia.

The Kratchmans were highly verbal, witty, and full of vitality. My father was treated cordially by his wife's large family, and they were very helpful in extending financial assistance when he suffered a heart attack and could not work for six months. I nevertheless always had the feeling that my father felt outnumbered by his wife's family. He was not averse to presenting himself in a self-promotional mode as better schooled in Jewish liturgy and politics. Despite my father's struggle to earn respect, I sensed a fair degree of harmony among family members, with everyone sharing the same Zionistic aspirations for a Jewish homeland.

There was one area where our Fanshel family differed from the Kratchmans. All of my cousins were in families where there were two offspring—a favored number in lower middle-class families—but my parents had four children, plus the daughter who had died on the boat coming over from Europe. The distinction of our family's size was not openly discussed when the extended families got together for social gatherings. However, I vaguely understood that our larger household was seen by my mother's siblings as contributing to the economic problems of our family. We lived in tight quarters on the fifth floor of an older building in the East Bronx. My having been born at home 1½ years after my brother Jack fits in with my overall picture of the straitened circumstances of my mother's experience in her maternal career.

I subconsciously had a sense that our large-sized family had left some emotional scars upon my mother. It came out in her somewhat vague references that "men had to be served," stated not as good-natured joshing about sex, but rather the voice of the oppressed female at a time when birth control was not available. It may have been the case that the Kratchman families were able to contain family size by more competently availing themselves of modern family planning. I would get a whiff of anti-masculine bitterness stated in indirect ways. I observed that men who showed an active interest in sex were sometimes described by my mother as *Huntem* ("animals").

My mother was born in 1890 in a small village in the Ukraine, not far from the city of Odessa. She was the second oldest of the five Kratchman children. Atypically for the Jewish population in the region, the family owned a modest farm and depended for income on the crops grown on their own land. Non-Jews surrounded them. Although living in an otherwise confining social world, the Kratchmans had contact with their non-Jewish neighbors when engaged in the sale of agricultural products and the purchase of goods and services.

When Clara was seven years old, her family enrolled her in the local Ukrainian school. Having received prior tutoring at home, she qualified for placement in the third grade. She found the

Clara Kratchman as a Young Woman

newness of the classroom environment intimidating, and this was aggravated by her awareness that she was the only Jewish child in the class. Her uneasiness was intensified when she became the target of derogatory taunts from her classmates. The teacher encouraged the rowdy behavior by frequently injecting scornful remarks about Jews in his presentations to the class.

Before long, Clara's sense of impending doom reached a climax. Provoked when Yiddish words inadvertently entered her response to a question about a topic they were discussing, the teacher struck her hands with a heavy wooden pointer. This violence was accompanied by a rebuke that rang in her ears: "You must only speak *Russian!*" Clara's classmates howled with glee, particularly when the teacher mimicked her offending words with a shrill rise-fall intonation suggestive of the Yiddish dialect. On returning home, Clara cried as she gave her father a description of the day's unhappy experiences. She expressed a determination to never again attend the school.

After considerable family discussion, it was agreed that Clara had been abused in a hostile school environment and ought to be spared further experiences of this kind. But the decision to withdraw her and to provide home tutoring had a sad underlay. The family realized that their lack of financial resources would make it difficult to recruit a qualified person to teach her. It was likely that the change would deprive Clara of the formal schooling that was the hallmark of an educated person.

With the loss of opportunity to attend school, Clara became a homebody. Despite her young age, and because she was readily available, she was increasingly called upon to assist in domestic chores. Treatment as a quasi-servant developed as a way of life in Clara's teens, when her father married a younger woman, following the death of his first wife.

Clara married Hyman Fanshel about 1914, when she was twenty-four years old. He came from a nearby town, where his father was the owner of a modest wool-shrinking business. Hyman was far better educated than his wife, having been provided with extended education in a school conducted under Jewish auspices. The experience made him worldly.

The Fanshel Family in Russia: Top row (left to right): *Sam Kratchman, Clara Kratchman Fanshel, Hyman Fanshel, Sonia Kratchman.* Bottom row (left to right): *Geitel Fanshel, the Author's Grantparents, and a Child Believed to Have Died.* In foregound, *Sol Fanshel, Dressed in White.*

I was never told how my father and mother met, what attracted them to each other, or why they decided to get married. I did not know whether their families knew each other or the degree to which they supported the union of my parents. While it is hard for me to believe—since such practices were not familiar to me as an American child—it is remotely possible that they were brought together by a *Shadchun* ("matchmaker"). Clara's age of twenty-four (Hyman was the same age) may have been considered rather late for a woman to marry, and perhaps she felt compelled to accept a proposal of marriage.

I never saw a display of affection between my parents, whether a buss on the cheek, a romantic kiss, an embrace, or any playful interaction between them. There were no verbal cues showing how they felt about each other or any facial gestures or body language that suggested the presence of a sense of romance. This absence of signs of love may have been a reflection of cultural norms, shyness, or the absence of physical attraction. Since I was not significantly exposed to other modes of couple interaction among the families I knew, I assumed that the arid quality of the interplay between my parents was the universal way fathers and mothers were supposed to relate to each other. It is probably no accident that when I got married and had children I would try to be open in displaying the romantic aspect of my relationship with my wife, Florence, often greeting her with a kiss when arriving at home after a day at work and using terms of endearment in my greeting, such as "dear," "honey," and "sweetie." This was genuinely felt, and the practice reflected my earlier uneasiness in living in a household where I was unsure whether my parents felt anything resembling affection for each other.

I was forty-five years old when my father died. He succumbed to a heart attack while sitting in the living room talking to my mother. I responded to my mother's emergency call and immediately drove to my parents' home. I remember being somewhat surprised to see my mother weeping. It seemed to be the first time I had witnessed a gesture that indicated love for my father. On reflection, I came to recognize the absurdity of my reaction. Just thinking of the many years in which their lives had been intertwined could easily evoke tears.

Mom took her responsibilities as a mother seriously. We children knew that she cared about each of us (and, later, our spouses and children) in a manner that avoided any aura of favoritism. True, my sister, Ruth, received special attention, but her brothers accepted the validity of the investment of time and energy in her. We understood that being the youngest child, the only representative of her gender among the four of us, and a replacement for the two-year-old daughter who had died on the boat bringing the family to the United States, made Ruth precious, and we shared in the great value placed on her presence in our midst.

Mom also had an eye for what was happening with the other relatives that constituted our extended Kratchman clan of five immigrant families. They helped us more frequently than we were called on to assist them, particularly after my father's heart attack when I was thirteen years old. But when Clara's older sister's husband, Morris Winitt, suffered a massive stroke and spent several years in a residence facility in the Bronx, it was rare for my parents to let a week go by without visiting him and the sister (Bluma) at home, bringing food and other items to make life easier for each of them.

Looking back at the way the emergent needs of families were met by mutual assistance efforts among them, I vividly remember Mom's being able to convince her youngest brother, Sam Kratchman, and his wife, Dora, to accept her offer of help in an important area of their family's life. She desired to spare their two boys—Ozzie and Jackie, both in their early teens—from having to spend summer days in New York City deprived of adequate recreation and to allow them to escape from the intense summer heat and doldrums. It was bad enough that Sam sweated six days a week in his hand laundry, dealing with an upper-class clientele living in the tall elevator buildings that surrounded his store. Dora helped him by folding sheets and garments. So in the midst of a particularly blistering summer, Mom proposed taking the two Kratchman boys with her when she and the three youngest Fan-

Aunt Bluma and Uncle Morris Winitt

shel children (Jack, myself, and Ruth) abandoned the Bronx for the cooler breezes and swimming opportunities at the seashore in Coney Island.

Responding to an advertisement spotted by my father in his Jewish-language newspaper, my mother had rented for the summer period half the space of a cottage occupied year-round by a needle tradesman and his family. The Bratzlavsky family's home was located two blocks from the seashore where people came from all over the city to swim.

With the Bratzlavsky family containing three children, two girls and a boy, the need to add to the family's cash income made it expedient to earn rental income during the summer months. It was a seasonal arrangement that required two families to live under quite crowded conditions.

My memory of the experience is that it was the diplomatic self-discipline of the women involved in the rental transaction that made the unusual shared-housing arrangement viable. Mom and Mrs. Bratzlavsky gave each other a wide berth in the kitchen, sharing a modest-sized refrigerator (it may have been an old-fashioned icebox), and, from all appearances, the two women even seemed to enjoy each other's company. The families ate in the kitchen in a two-stage sequence.

Weather permitting, the Fanshel and Kratchman youth were outdoors a great deal. A nearby schoolyard provided a venue for Jack and Ozzie to play long hours of basketball day in and day out. The younger children found the long boardwalk along the beach a great place to roam and thus also escaped the cramped feeling generated by the crowded quarters.

The big challenge came on the weekends, when Pop as well as Uncle Sam and Aunt Dora joined us in the important task of allowing family members to reconnect and feel whole again. Coming from a very close family, it was obviously important for Ozzie and Jackie to have direct contact with their parents on weekends. As I look back, I find myself wondering how four adults and five youngsters managed to sleep in the not-so-large two-bedroom space we occupied. My memory is that we all slept crosswise in the beds instead of lengthwise, with two beds having to absorb the

Uncle Irving Kratchman and Aunt Sonia Kratchman [Kaplan]

load of three or four bodies. That the beds did not collapse still strikes me as a miracle!

The arrangement was so successful that Ozzie and Jackie joined us for a repeat of the routine during two succeeding summers. And sometimes our ranks were joined by other extended family members who came out to spend the day with us in Coney Island.

Mom had to deal with special issues in settling in the United States when the family arrived in 1920. She was unable to speak English, but she also was handicapped because she had had very little formal education as a child. Over the years, my mother made a masterful effort to become competent in the English language. This enabled her to write to her three sons when we were in military service in World War II. Later in life, she was able to write home to her children and grandchildren when she and my father went on trips. She also became famous for the little reminder notes left around her home, with all kinds of words or sayings she was attempting to incorporate into her communication in the English language. She jotted down new words on the backs of envelopes or whatever other paper was available. She had an ear for comments she heard while sitting on buses or in the subway, or observed in advertisements to be looked up later in her dictionary.

My wife, Florence, and I were delighted and impressed when we were vacationing in Massachusetts while my wife was recuperating from surgery to get a letter from Mom asking about her daughter-in-law's state of recovery. My mother concluded her report of local goings-on with information about the weather in New York with this endearing sign-off: "The weather has been fine, with intermittent showers"—straight off the corner of the front page of the New York *Times*.

A Group of Zionist Youth to which Hyman (far right with moustache) Belonged.

4

Hyman Fanshel

From early childhood, my father's social world was narrowly confined to individuals like himself. Interaction with non-Jews took place on a fairly regular basis, but such contacts exclusively served the purpose of buying and selling goods and services. My father's outlook was influenced by the organized mistreatment of Jews in the late nineteenth and early twentieth centuries, particularly those manifest during his early youth. I would often hear him recount the brutal massacre that had taken place in Kishinev in 1903 when he was thirteen years old. It lasted for three days, and some forty-seven Jews were killed and almost a hundred severely wounded. The assault was in retaliation for the alleged murder of a Christian Russian boy, whose death by Ukrainian nationalists was attributed to the age-old blood libel against the Jews. It was said that the boy had been killed to use his blood in the preparation of Passover matzo. My father could recite the names of many other pogroms—involving the planned extermination of Jews sanctioned by government—taking place in eastern Europe.

The specter of anti-Semitism that my father's family faced became personalized for me when he recounted the experience of my paternal grandfather, who earned his livelihood as a wool-shrinker. My grandfather's interaction with non-Jews was reserved for the purpose of receiving wool shorn from their sheep so the accumulated raw materials could be made fit for sale to manufacturers of clothing. Sometime during my father's teen years, my grandfather suffered a catastrophe when a large consignment of wool left for shrinking by a group of Ukrainian customers was stolen in the middle of the night. My grandfather's life was threatened if he did not rectify the situation and compensate his customers for their losses. As a result, he had to borrow considerable funds from family and friends to pay his antagonists, and he became burdened with a staggering debt.

My grandfather made the difficult decision to go to the United States where he could get employment to earn the money he now owed. He labored for several years at a shop in New York City where animal slaughterers and meat packers were employed in assembly-line fashion. His absence from the family was keenly felt.

This story about my grandfather intrigued me, because I had otherwise been given no account of this important forebear. The thought of him as a muscular man carrying animal carcasses in defense of his family gave me a feeling of pride, because the image of Jewish men playing out manly roles had never been conveyed to me by my parents.

My father had warm relationships with men now scattered around the world whom he had known in his youth. After he emigrated to the United States, he determinedly maintained a correspondence with these friends. I often observed him on Sunday mornings sitting by himself at the kitchen table absorbed in writing to friends who had remained in Russia or had emigrated to many places, including Argentina, Cuba, Palestine, and France. He took pride in the elegance of his Yiddish writing—indeed, his script was quite artistic—and would sometimes read to my mother the content of a letter he had composed. She was always an interested listener and clearly admired Pop's writing skills. I also enjoyed hearing his eloquent words, and I grasped that in the context of the friendships going back to his early years in Russia, my father could be a warmer, more gracious person than the more taciturn one we children often experienced. It was only well into my adulthood that I could overcome the wariness he aroused in me.

Among the artifacts left behind after my parents died—my father in 1967 at age seventy-seven and my mother in 1978 at age eighty-eight—was an old photograph of my father and six of his friends in Russia (page 46). This picture of Hyman and his friends moved me. It was as if I could read the idealism on their faces.

Based upon past conversations with my father, I wouldn't be surprised if the group of young men shown in the photograph had been talking about their aspirations to leave Russia some day and settle in the area around Jerusalem. My father told me that they enjoyed learning about the culture of the Jewish people in poetry, story writing, and theatre.

My father's favorite Jewish poet was Chaim Nachman Bialik, who was particularly revered because he revived Hebrew as a living language. Here is how the poet is described by Ruth Nevo in *Bialik: Caught in a World Whose God Is Dead*:

> [Bialik] shared [Hebrew essayist] Ahad Ha'am's stringent criticism of Jewish apathy and many of the conflicting and sterile trends in political Zionism of the time; and a considerable number of his poems are searing denunciations, in prophetic vein, of his people's shortcomings. In "The City of Slaughter," written after the pogrom of 1903 in Kishinev, he excoriated the victims, rather than the pogromists, for the craven dishonor of their loss of human dignity; and the poem, vitriolic in its fierce exposure, played a considerable part in the development of a new national will to self-defense.

My father was toughened in his outlook by identifying strongly with Bialik and other highly politicized intellectuals. By the time I came upon the scene three years after the Fanshels arrived in America, his investment in the survival of the Jews was total. When witness to similar phenomena in the United States—for example, Jews being ostracized and barred from certain social settings, professions, or even securing a room at a hotel—he was angered to think of all the difficulty he and his family had gone through to get to America, only to find signs of the anti-Semitic hostility he had suffered in the Ukraine.

Hyman invested his total being in his Jewish identification. This emphasis in his life provided the major defense against the hateful forces he encountered, particularly in his formative years in Czarist Russia. Early on, he learned that the pogrom-makers were out to kill the Jews, and this fact ate at him. It was his belief that Jews should not allow themselves to be unresisting victims supinely yielding to their oppressors, but band together and hold on to their identity. All other concerns had to be subordinated to one's self-identity as a Jew. Only by recognizing such passion could one understand a man who sought to make certain that after he died his tombstone would bear the inscription *He Was a Devoted Zionist.*

My father sometimes revealed himself as an assertive Jew in small social gestures, putting himself forth in a manner that gave me a hint of his thinking. I recall occasions in my preteen years when he and I would be sitting together on a New York subway train. He would open up his newspaper, *Der Tag ("The Day")*, and hold it spread in front of his face with the Yiddish script boldly emblazoned on the front page for all to see. He was a cool guy, ignoring how others might react to him. At the time, I did not know whether to be proud of my father for his fearlessness or critical because he was bringing attention to himself in a way that obviously turned others off. You could almost read the fear on the faces of other passengers that people like my father were not fitting in.

Hyman was not the only one displaying his Jewishness in public. At age twelve, I walked through subway cars holding a Jewish National Fund money collection can known as a *Pushkeh* ("little box for coins"). I would call out for funds to be donated to facilitate the settlement of Jews in Palestine. The assignment was given me by the teachers at the Jacob H. Schiff Center, and my parents approved my being given this task. I managed to force myself to carry out the fund-raising, but felt awkward about presenting myself in this manner.

Our father's penchant for using our religious identity as a guide to living was the focus of his concerns as he developed rules for us children to follow. As a young child, I could not make sense of the fact that my father would raise a fuss if he discerned that a new friend of mine was not Jewish, and I would invariably be admonished to avoid playing with the *goyim* ("gentiles"). He had learned to hate the non-Jews who created murderous pogroms against the Jews in Russia, and he continued to regard all gentiles with suspicion after arriving in the United States.

My mother was inclined to defer to Hyman's lead in defining appropriate ways for their children to conduct themselves in preserving their Jewish identity. He clearly had more schooling, and the tradition among Russian Jews tended to support the view that fathers should carry the major responsibility for guiding offspring in the ways of the Jewish people. She also supported him because his decision-making in these areas reflected the beliefs of the family in which she had grown up.

Indicative of his strong affirmation of who we were, the identification of the Fanshel children as Jews was established when we were born by assigning biblical names to each of us: Saul, Jacob, David, and Ruth. Of course, liberties were taken in adapting our names, so that these got transformed over time to the diminutive renderings Sol, Yankel, Duvid, and Rootie. Sometimes this practice was the stimulus for derision by friends for whom Yiddish-sounding names seemed quite funny. I was caught up short one day, however, when I was twelve years old, and Jack—a head taller than me—grabbed me by the collar and almost choked me to death. He shouted in my ear that if I called him "Yankel" again —or "Jakie" for that matter— he would "beat the shit" out of me. I understood that he meant his threat, and I never called him by either name again.

The household in which we grew up was very much flavored by our origins. I mean *flavor* literally. The food we ate and the associated cooking odors you might detect in approaching our apartment door in the Bronx clearly identified us as a Russian-Jewish household. You might know the stuff: borscht, matzo ball soup, knishes, stuffed cabbage, and so forth. Go to Sammy's Rumanian Restaurant in New York City, and you'll find these and other ethnic dishes well represented on the menu.

Three languages comprised our family's repertoire for routine conversation: Yiddish, Russian, and English. My parents talked to their four kids in Yiddish, and we responded in English. Back and forth in our separate languages, the generations managed to understand each other. My parents conversed in Russian when they wanted to keep secrets from us. Later in my life, when I occasionally saw Russian movies, I found the sounds of this familiar but not-understood language pleasing to my ear. And when my siblings and I spoke in English to each other, our parents were sometimes confused about what was going on. This met a need we had to gain some control over our lives.

A recurrent theme in the history of the Fanshel family was the struggle my three siblings and I had in establishing our individual lifestyles and personal goals in the face of our father's decided views on many social questions. Hyman's resort to authoritarian controls as he sought to shape our lives—often regarded as arbitrary by us and resisted—was demonstrated in important areas and in trivial matters as well. As the oldest, Sol had his struggles in seeking to emancipate himself, and he experienced great anguish in dealing with our father as he tried to chart his life course as a college student and beyond. And with Jack, the next oldest child, there was again an unambiguous display of authoritarianism being played out. Jack's inability to obtain parental approval for participation in his high school basketball team typified the destructive impact of Hyman's rule by edict. Jack's encounter with our father was a demoralizing experience, with the contentious matter being resolved by my brother's self-destructive decision to quit high school—a scenario that eventually led to him not finishing high school, while his three siblings became college graduates and earned doctoral degrees.

Hyman gave marching orders and expected to be obeyed. In doing so, he often came across as mean-spirited, very much a despot. In my adulthood, I see him as probably driven by his difficulty in coping with the American environment. But the cause could also have been deeper. Clearly, there was something in his makeup that prevented our father from being sensitive to the needs of his children and unable to give them any opportunity for personal decision-making as they tried to shape their futures. As I wonder about the sources of this conduct, I focus on the hint of religious orthodoxy and the larger meaning of his Jewishness in his own growing-up experiences. These may have provided a template for the oppressive style of his paternal performance. Even a seemingly innocent matter such as an avid interest in sports, as shown by Jack, could be viewed as a distraction from the more important Jewish agenda. It was clearly defined by Hyman as a diversionary and alien influence.

It needs to be said that our father had a lesser investment in the matter of our religiosity, and that he could even make peace with our being atheists, although he probably disliked the word intensely as an empty modern affectation. What he sought to insure was that his children felt connected with the Jewish people in a very active and committed way.

Although he was spurred by noble motivations, the trouble for the family was that Hyman's approach relied on coercion and was thoroughly heavy-handed. In my case, it felt as if he was trying to shove the centrality of being Jewish down my throat. He was unable to moderate his demands by using a more gentle and affectionate style of conveying his sentiments. Sadly, his bullying methods undermined his intention to affect our thinking.

From the distance of time, I find it possible to look back at the distress my siblings and I experienced with our father and engage in a process of reflection that permits some reduction of my angst. In my father's contacts with old friends and extended family, I witnessed responses to him from people that indicated that they held him in high regard and indeed felt affection for him.

The West Washington Market, Manhattan, 1936, Where Hyman Made His Daily Produce Pick-up. (Photo by Berenice Abbot, Photography collections, Miriam and Ira D. Wallach Division of Art, Prints and Photographs, The New York Public Library, Astor, Lenox and Tilden Foundations)

5

Thanksgiving in the Bronx, 1936

Although as a thirteen-year-old I was hardly in tune with the social issues percolating in the country, I was hearing talk about something called the "Depression" in the Bronx neighborhood where I lived, and the grim reality of life around us began to enter my awareness. Human misery confronted us unmistakably when we saw families being evicted from their apartments for nonpayment of rent and tough-looking men hired by landlords dumping the furnishings of these luckless families onto the sidewalks in front of their buildings.

My sense of the abnormality of the times became vivid when a school friend informed me one day that he changed his address every month. His family's unique survival strategy took advantage of a landlord's offer of a month's "concession" of free rent if the family moved into a vacant apartment. When the rent-free period was over, the family would move in the middle of the night to a different apartment building where the same opportunity for freeloading could take place.

Anxiety about the lack of a decent cash income hung over our family like a cumulous cloud. My mother had the burden of feeding her four children in addition to Hyman and herself on a barely adequate household allowance. She diligently managed to meet the family's basic needs, and we never experienced hunger.

I realized that one way Clara rose to the challenge was by performing magic tricks with cheap foods, using the cooking skills she had learned as a youngster on a farm in the Ukraine. For example, using the damaged fruit brought home by my father because it did not meet the standard of appearance required by his store owner customers, Mom turned out the most delicious fruit pies one could hope for. She also bought cheap cuts of meat, marinating them until they were as tender as filet mignon. Eating at our dinner table, you would sometimes think we were dining at a fancy restaurant.

We also benefited from a helping network within our extended family. With two of my uncles owning grocery stores, we received, on a weekly basis, dozens of cracked eggs and those rejected in the candling process because they had blood spots, objectionable in Jewish dietary practice. With a big sack of flour thrown in, Clara baked up a storm, and loaves of challah bread, a favorite among Jewish families, were distributed to nearby households in our Fanshel-Kratchman network. This made Friday nights more festive to celebrate the onset of the sabbath.

I was accidentally provided a glimpse of another way in which Clara met the cash needs to maintain our household. I was surprised one day to witness her tiptoeing into my parents' bedroom where Hyman was sleeping. He routinely needed to rest when he returned in mid-afternoon from a tiring workday that began at 4 A.M. I saw her take from a dresser drawer a brown paper bag packed with money belonging to my father. In it was the accumulation of the day's sales receipts my father had collected when he delivered produce to the stores using his services. The money represented the capital required for the next day's purchases to accommodate incoming orders.

Without hesitation, Mom helped herself to some cash. I gathered that she regarded the money bag as joint property and not just my father's to control. I felt awed by her audacity in performing this clandestine action and was impressed with the cool nerve she showed in foraging in what Pop considered his private reserve.

I understood that the mission accomplished that very afternoon resulted in my sister, Ruthie, obtaining the pair of shoes my mother felt she required.

Later in the day, Hyman picked up his bag and did a quick assessment of his assets. His face tightened with anger as he confronted my mother and accused her of appropriating money from his improvised purse while he was sleeping. After a pause in which my mother mobilized her defense, I was fascinated to see her look him straight in the eyes and firmly contest him with a zinger: *"Du bist a ligner"* ("You are a liar").

I later decided that my parents had an unacknowledged understanding. Clara would maintain the family within the grossly inadequate allowance made available to her, but this could be augmented when she was under intense financial strain by additional funds obtained from his money bag while my father was sleeping. I thought this a strange arrangement, but it was incontrovertible that Mom had no other way to buy new shoes for my sister. In my innocence, I wondered why my father could not take it upon himself to just give her the money since she was obviously not filching it to have a good time. But I soon gave up trying to fathom the domestic arrangements under which we Fanshels lived.

Unfortunately, I was influenced by this strange family phenomenon. I found myself on occasion seized by a compulsion to enter my parents' bedroom while Hyman was sleeping for the purpose of helping myself to a handful of change. Some goings-on! In the inner recesses of my heart, I felt shame that I was becoming a delinquent. As far as I am aware, I was the only one of the Fanshel children to engage in this larcenous behavior.

To ease the economic squeeze on our family, and also because he had a strong urge to be independent, my twenty-one-year-old brother, Sol, moved out of our apartment to live on his own. He had graduated from City College earlier in the year. Nevertheless, his departure was a bit of a shocker and disrupted the cohesion of the household.

My parents were not sympathetic to my brother's show of independence. They were apprehensive that our relatives would think that the move had been precipitated by a family quarrel.

They also felt that since Sol had prospects for earning income as a recently graduated electrical engineer, his continuing to live at home would actually improve our economic circumstances rather than constitute a burden.

Sol's decision to share living quarters with a man who was an artist of Japanese descent added to the coolness of my parents' attitude. His living with someone from a race of people outside their life experience was disturbing to them and evoked a fear that Sol was becoming a Bohemian. Their viewpoint was revealed in the way they questioned Sol, and this sign of what he considered racial intolerance further alienated my brother from our parents, being at odds with the political radicalization he had undergone in college.

With Sol out of our home, there were now three children remaining. But with five people to feed, the Fanshels still required more dough-re-mi. As a way of dealing with the pressure, Hyman added to his workload by taking on more customers. This may not have been wise, because he often labored for long hours each day. He showed signs of being stressed beyond his endurance, and my mother appeared to be worried about him. How much more could he take? she wondered.

My father's principal earnings came from making wholesale purchases for fruits and vegetables on order from a dozen clients, all retail store proprietors. His work was made possible by the ownership of a worn but still operational truck. He was proud of owning even a used Brockway, produced by the well-known company that had been a significant supplier of military vehicles in World War I. He also took pride in his status as an entrepreneur, and liked to refer to himself as a "wholesaler." Unfortunately, it was a highly competitive business, and he operated with an element of uncertainty, because the store owners could be fickle in their loyalties. They were always being made counteroffers by my father's competitors, who claimed they could provide better-quality produce at lower prices.

Every night before going to bed, Hyman telephoned each of his customers to take their orders for the next day's deliveries. As he took notes during these telephone conversations, he would repeat the orders: "Three boxes of lettuce, a bag of onions, two boxes of celery . . . " and so forth. When my father finished calling the stores, he would telephone the information to the wholesale merchants at the Washington Market, New York City's huge produce distribution center, to facilitate loading his truck when he arrived. In these telephone calls, I could often hear him berate his suppliers for the poor quality of their recent sales to him: "Joe, those strawberries you sold me were rotten through and through. You put nice ones on top of the *farfoylter* ("putrid") ones." I was taken aback later to learn that my father often reprimanded the people he made purchases from, even when what they had sold him had actually been in good condition. "Keeps them on their toes," he exclaimed with an air of self-satisfaction.

The following day, Hyman would get up in the dark hours of the morning to drive into Manhattan to the Washington Market. The groans my father usually made as he struggled out of bed at 4 A.M. penetrated our apartment. This always reinforced my awareness of his miserable work life. His noisy awakenings startled me out of my sleep and created the melancholy feeling that I had just had a bad dream. Even on Sundays, when he was not working, he seemed to be in a constant state of exhaustion.

Hyman did much of the heavy lifting of the produce bags and boxes onto the truck himself, and his noisy wheezing and grunts suggested that he was not up to the physical strain. He reminded those of us who witnessed his labors that he used to be a white-collar worker in Russia and was not destined to be a man who worked with the brawn of his back. When he had sufficient funds, he would recruit a paid day laborer from among the unemployed men who hung out at the Market.

The irony is that, despite the stress he put himself under, Hyman did not earn enough money to adequately take care of the family's needs. As a source of additional income during the fall of 1936, my father entered into partnership with two friends to operate the recently opened Ideal Fruit and Vegetable Emporium, a store located in the Marble Hill area of Manhattan around 225th Street. He characterized his involvement as something called a "silent partner," performing services for the enterprise about which I knew nothing. I could see that my father was excited about increasing our income.

I was aware that my parents quarreled a great deal about money. When I saw them arguing about this, I would become antsy and often run out of the house to join my friends. So I hoped my father would succeed in this new venture and get our family out of our financial pinch. I silently cheered him on from the sidelines: *"Go to it, Pop! Be a success in America!"*

Hyman told Clara that the new store was busy with customers shopping for the Thanksgiving holiday. They were coming in crowds to buy potatoes, chestnuts, cranberries, and other fixings that go with what was probably the most elaborately prepared meal of the year for most American families. The turkey was, of course, the centerpiece of the occasion, and he told us that more of these large birds were purchased for this one holiday than for the rest of the year combined. Clara had already put in her order with Moshe, the butcher on 183rd Street, which meant that our Russian Jewish family would fit in with the rest of the country. I later found out that my mother had actually ordered a goose. Cheaper and, she assured us, "Just as good as a turkey." Clearly, cutting corners in her spending was the way she got the Fanshel children properly fed and clothed.

The store's cash register was ringing like mad, and Hyman liked the sound of it. There was a surge in the demand for home deliveries, as the neighborhood women were buying more than they could carry. The store's regular delivery boy was out sick, and the burden had fallen on Tony Mondello. He was the sole hired clerk, single, twenty-five years old, and from a Sicilian family. His main task was to unload the produce from my father's truck when his orders were delivered from Washington Market. In addition to putting out the fruits and vegetables for display each day, Tony waited on customers when the two partners were busy.

The heavy load of delivering orders placed a strain upon Tony, who could not get around easily because of a physical handicap. I had heard him referred to as a "cripple" because he had a limp, and one of his shoes had a sole about two inches thick. Everyone felt protective of him because he never complained. When I got to meet Tony, I found that I liked him right away because of his gentle and easy manner. Looking at his handsome face, I was confirmed in my opinion that Italians and Jews were very similar in how they approached people. They were unlike the Irish kids who attended the Our Lady of Refuge Catholic School in my neighborhood. These roughnecks were referred to pejoratively as "micks," and we in turn were called "sheenies." Insulting each other was part of the street life we led, and my antagonists handed me my lumps on occasion. They invariably let me know that the Jews killed Christ, and that I had been chosen to pay for this crime. I sometimes could retaliate physically when there were not too many to fight. I was generally wary of them.

Hyman was in a state of high excitement because his business venture was going to pay off with more money for the family. In an expansive spirit, he let his partners know that Tony was carrying too much of the load and that he had decided to volunteer my services as a delivery boy to fill in during this holiday period. He did so knowing that this would keep me out of school for a few days. The partners were told that I was thirteen years old and could be relied upon to do the job well: "Davie's a good boy."

There was no consulting with me about the matter, because the business needed someone, and my brother Jack, who was employed in the garment district, was not available. When Hyman detected a lack of enthusiasm in my response to his offer of my services, he reprimanded me sharply in a physically threatening way. "You are old enough to work, and I can't do everything by myself. You'll come with me to the store tomorrow morning. And that is *that*." There was no inquiry as to whether I had anything scheduled, or something I might want to do recreationally that was important to me. My earlier concern that my father seemed to be exhausted at the end of each workday evaporated in the face of my indignation.

My father figured that I would make good tips and that, in addition to earning extra spending money, I could help the family finance the purchase of a roll-away bed for my sister, Ruthie.

Friends and relatives often remarked that she should not have to continue sleeping on the living room couch, which had served as her bed for years. My mother would say: "By all rights, she should have a bed. After all, she's a girl and needs privacy." This thinking struck me as for the birds. I thought: "Why the hell should I be buying furniture for my sister?" I reasoned that furniture came with the house, and kids like me didn't buy such stuff.

I was frankly pissed off. I had planned to get together with my friends to play basketball in the Jacob H. Schiff Center gym. We had been planning to practice for the Center tournament that was coming up. Besides, it was cold and raining, and I did not look forward to delivering orders all day. I reckoned I'd probably freeze my ass off. But when I began to protest, my father gave me one of his withering looks, and out of a sense of self-preservation, I retreated from any attempt to argue further with him. I reluctantly went along with my new assignment.

So there I was, the newly recruited delivery boy at the Ideal Fruit and Vegetable Emporium. The work turned out to be even more atrocious than I had anticipated. I was on the run the entire day and felt lucky if I could take time to go to the bathroom. Most of the time I loaded the delivery cart until it was full of heavy bags, making about six deliveries on a single trip, and trod my way through the streets looking for addresses and entrances to houses. I often had to go through basements that were invariably filthy with roaches and mice crawling around. It was necessary to hoist the bags up dumbwaiters whose coarse ropes often had splinters that penetrated my gloves. I was also worried that my cart would be stolen, so I had to be careful to put it under lock and key each time I delivered an order.

By midday, I was exhausted and my clothes, wet from rain and sweat, were clinging uncomfortably to my body. My shoes made squishy sounds as I walked in the flooded streets. Cold and sneezing, I felt sorry for myself and was sure that I was running a temperature. Although healthy and physically strong enough to perform the work, I built up a feeling of antagonism against my father for subjecting me to what I considered to be a disgusting experience. None of my friends were being put through the hoops like this, and my thoughts were filled with venom. *"What the hell kind of father is Hyman anyway? Why is he such a mean bastard?"* Fuming and fussing in an internal dialogue with my father, I managed to complete the day.

After finishing work, Hyman and I went home together. We took hot baths to clean up before dinner. I enjoyed lingering in the warm bathwater and could feel the accumulated chill of the day's delivery chores leave my body. My mood lifted as I felt myself relaxing.

Characteristically, my mother took her responsibility for feeding us seriously. She had prepared a large meal, including appetizers, soup, chicken, and potatoes, with honey cake for dessert. I was included in the anointed category of *der menner* ("the men") of the family who had been laboring all day and required attentive care by the housewife. This treatment permitted me to experience myself as manly. More than at my bar mitzvah initiation, I could now say: "Today I am a man." Despite my grievances, I was impressed with my new status, and was possibly even warmed by the treatment I received.

When the meal was over, though, I managed to rekindle my sense of injustice about what my father had put me through. *"Such a tyrant. It would serve him right if he broke a leg!"*

We somehow got through the Thanksgiving holidays, and I no longer had to go to the store for delivery work. But as the Christmas season approached, my father again found himself under great pressure from his expanded work commitments. And then came a catastrophe.

It had snowed heavily all night. The evening before, we knew that very bad weather had been predicted. When Hyman went to work this one morning, the accumulated snow was piled high, and it was still snowing. The whistling of the wind indicated that it was probably bitterly cold outside.

As usual, Mr. Bezinsky, the garage owner with whom Hyman entrusted his truck, had arranged for the vehicle to be delivered to the front of our apartment house at about four o'clock in the morning. A second car took the driver back to the garage.

I could hear my father getting up in the darkness and letting out his usual blood-curdling groans as he did. After awhile, I heard him close the door on his way to work and I returned to a sound sleep.

Suddenly, the stillness of the predawn was dramatically interrupted as the family was abruptly awakened by a loud banging on our apartment door and an insistent ringing of the bell. When my mother asked in a frightened voice, "Who's there?" she learned that a policeman had come to tell us some shocking news. Hyman had been found prostrate in the snow in front of his truck. The police had taken him to the emergency room at the local hospital, accompanied by a relative.

My mother made an emergency call to Dr. Isaac Brodsky, our long-time family doctor, with whom my mother conversed in Yiddish; he was an old friend whose roots in Russia were the same as my parents'. It was determined that Hyman had experienced a major, life-threatening heart attack. Arrangements were made at once for Clara to go to the hospital.

The police who had come upon the scene surmised that what probably happened was that my father was unable to start his truck in the freezing weather. His efforts to energize the motor by rotating the crankshaft manually were apparently very difficult because of the bitter cold. Dr. Brodsky was of the opinion that a major vessel had torn in Hyman's chest, creating a massive heart attack. The subzero temperature not only made turning the crank extremely difficult, it also stiffened the arteries in my father's heart, a classic precursor to a calamity.

After a week's treatment to stabilize his condition, my father was taken off the hospital's critical list and plans were made for him to convalesce at home. Dr. Brodsky revealed the full nature of the disaster when he decided that Hyman would have to be restricted to bed rest for six months while his heart healed. This was a misfortune of enormous dimensions. How would the family manage to keep going financially without my father being able to make a living?

My father's return from the hospital after two weeks was the first ray of sunshine we had experienced since his heart attack.

It felt like normalcy was returning, even though he was going to be restricted to bed for a long time. The relatives visited in droves until Dr. Brodsky called a halt to their presence, admonishing them that the patient required peace and quiet if he was to regain his health. As it was, Hyman would probably never be able to resume his truck-driving occupation, because it would likely result in a second heart attack.

Now that he had been close to death, I began to feel stirrings of concern for my father. His being in a vulnerable state for the first time in my life took away the aura of invincibility in which I had always seen him. He was no longer all-powerful, to be experienced as a frequent source of oppression and arbitrary control of my life. This tilt in my feelings prompted me to recall how I had cursed him to myself as I was delivering fruit and vegetable orders in the rain. In reaction to my having been drenched and shivering with cold, I had wished that he would break a leg or something worse. The "worse" had indeed happened, and I was mortified to realize that, by some magical power involved in cursing one's own parent, I had almost killed my father. No doubt about it, I had put the whammy on him, and my scandalous wish for his destruction had almost done him in!

An enormous sense of guilt took hold, making it hard to live with myself. I searched for ways to atone for my sins, but I was not successful in this pursuit. I felt like shit.

The Fanshel Family, circa 1931: Top row (left to right): *Sol, Clara, Hyman.* Bottom row (left to right): *David, Ruth, Jack.*

6

The Firstborn Son Returns

At twenty-one, having graduated from City College as an electrical engineer, my eldest brother, Sol, had recently succeeded in obtaining employment. He would be working with the WPA (Works Project Administration) as a surveyor on a public construction project that would create a new subway line for the city of New York.

My brother had long chafed at the limitations of living in our home. From his general demeanor and comments made in my presence, it had been clearly oppressive and confining for him to reside in a small apartment with his parents and younger siblings. Sleeping in the same room with his two younger brothers struck him as absurd, and he was chomping at the bit to be an independent adult, accountable only to himself.

More aggravating than the crowding had been the frequent arguments with Pop, who deemed it his right to assert his authority over any activity in which my brother might be engaged. Now that he had the opportunity to be getting out on his own, Sol felt upbeat in a way he never could before.

It had not been easy landing a job in the midst of a severe economic slump. The entire City College graduating class of engineers seemed adrift as they tried to find work. The scarcity of employment opportunities created such doubts about their prospects that a large group of students marched to the Soviet Embassy to apply for jobs in Russia. They had been told that opportunities were more promising for them in an emerging socialist economy determined to build an infrastructure from the ground up. The Depression had radicalized many of the children of recent immigrants attending New York City's premier free college, and they were ready to look far and wide for any job. In the end, the mass emigration did not take place because the federal government, under President Franklin Roosevelt's leadership, was creating new initiatives in public works, and jobs, such as the one Sol had just found, were suddenly being generated in the United States. Sol felt especially fortunate because many avenues of employment were closed to Jewish applicants.

Unfortunately, my brother was not fated to be happy long. The economic disaster that gripped our family following our father's heart attack affected him as well. His earnings were needed at home; family survival required him to give up the independence that had been so hard won. After a period of soul-searching, Sol submitted to the decision he felt the situation required of him, and he returned home to resume living in our apartment.

As distressing as it was for my brother to see our father laid low by a close-to-death experience, it was not easy to accept the situation in which he was now placed. He saw himself being asked to abandon his dreams.

I probably was too young to fully understand what was going on, but at some level of primitive comprehension I was made uncomfortable by the seismic changes taking place in the power relations within my family. This was particularly obvious in the sparring between my father and Sol. Since becoming a contributor to the family's income, my brother could now be more self-assertive in dealing with Hyman's authoritarian approach, and his responses to provocations reflected a readiness to challenge intrusions into his domain.

It was difficult for Sol to put aside the grievances he had accumulated. He had reason to wonder whether his going to college was fully supported by the family. It seemed to him that his success in earning a degree—a major achievement in our family—had been accomplished over the active resistance of my father. Sol particularly resented Hyman's frequent references to cousins who were going to evening school at City College. He was often told that, by working days, the Feldmans' four employed children could contribute necessary income to their families. "Not like Sol," rang unpleasantly in my brother's ears. It raised bitter feelings to hear himself rebuked for raising the household electric bills with late-night studying, which my father defined as being irresponsible in the use of the family's resources.

Because I, too, felt oppressed by my father's dictatorial approach to his children, although on a much less intense scale, it would have been logical for me to be rooting for my older brother as he sought to assert himself. But something was holding me back from having full sympathy with Sol in his struggle. Perhaps my being eight years his junior prevented me from conceiving a life apart from my parents in the way my more mature sibling could. With his engineering degree as a credential, Sol could make it on his own and could shake off the oppression he had experienced.

I wanted things to remain as they were before Hyman's heart attack. Even though I was very aware of my father's power over me, and intimidated when his anger was provoked, I did not want to see him weakened and have our family move into uncharted territory. The continuation of my father's authority provided the security that there was an underlying order to life in our family. The alternative would be chaos, and who knows what dangers such disarray would bring in an environment so full of anger? Although I did not reveal my feelings to Sol, I very much wished he would get into line and behave himself.

As I struggled to understand the unpleasantness of our family's situation, I realized that there was a deeper hurt. I was feeling personally rejected by the message Sol was giving out: *"I don't want to live with you guys anymore."* I felt consumed with questions: *"Why is he so determined to get out of our house? Doesn't he love us? Doesn't he know that I'm his biggest admirer, and that he is an important person in my life?"* I still looked upon him as my "big brother." And I was proud that he was our first college graduate! How could he think of abandoning us?

The antagonism festering beneath the surface in the encounters between my father and my brother became openly exposed when they talked about politics. Hyman made his feelings explicit: He hated the Communists in Russia with a passion that came from his personal experiences in the changes brought on by the October Revolution.

To earn his living in 1917, my father chose employment as a self-designated "middle man." He organized his own economic activity by purchasing large batches of coal from suppliers in the countryside and sold small quantities to customers in the Odessa area who used this fuel to heat their homes. Under the czar, this kind of enterprise had economic legitimacy and attracted minor Jewish entrepreneurs like my father, who were denied access to other forms of business. The money earned this way helped the Fanshel family stay alive. Under economic reforms introduced by the Bolsheviks, this type of business became defined as a "black market" activity and was outlawed. It was seen as a remnant of capitalism that was a drag upon the socialist society envisioned by the revolutionaries.

Hyman's determination to leave Russia arose from his experience in being caught continuing his illegal business activity in violation of the new regulations. Bad things happened when an informant reported him to the authorities, and he was ignominiously arrested as a "parasite" and jailed for several weeks. Given the responsibilities he carried as a husband and the father of two children, there was fear that Hyman would be imprisoned for years, even sent to Siberia. Luckily, a release from prison was achieved by friends who were able to bribe the officials in charge of his case.

Stung by the way he was labeled as a black marketeer by the new authorities, and convinced that he had been singled out for arrest because he was Jewish, Hyman felt unforgiving toward his tormentors. It stuck in his craw that he had even suffered the derogation by Communists of Jewish background who expressed their contempt for him as a *shtekel-drayer* ("cane twirler"). This designation was that of a man standing on a corner twirling a cane, Charlie Chaplin style, a signal that he was approachable for a "deal." The experience left Hyman with a bitter feeling, and mention of the subject of life under the Communists would provoke an outpouring of bitter denouncements of the Russian regime.

Equally galling to Hyman was his awareness that the Communists were strongly opposed to the principles of Zionism, particularly the concept of a Jewish return to their biblical land in Palestine. For Hyman, a socialistically oriented Zionist from his early youth, these views were the mainstay of his existence and provided him with a sense of his roots.

To Hyman's chagrin as he lay homebound for an extended period of rest after his heart attack, Sol was showing signs of being responsive to the thinking of the left. My father did not like hearing from his son that arranging the distribution of coal on a fair basis to all of the people, instead of selling it to the highest bidders for a profit, was eminently more reasonable. What my father defined as "enemy" thought was penetrating his own household, and he made it clear that such manifestations were not welcome in his home.

My brother had been introduced to radical ideas at City College and was particularly impressed by the widespread student activity on behalf of the Loyalists engaged in the defense of the Spanish Republic. A raging civil war had recently begun on the Iberian peninsula, and world attention seemed riveted to it. Some students were signing up with other Americans for the Abraham Lincoln Brigade to become part of the international military force being mobilized against fascism. Sol's understanding of the rightness of this struggle did not quite match Hyman's sense of priorities from a world perspective.

Ironically, my father was also expressing concern about the rise of a virulent anti-Semitic government in Germany led by Adolph Hitler, a German leader Hyman identified as very dangerous. The ominous international news had reminded him of the violent pogroms against the Jews in Russia that took place in his youth. My father could name every pogrom that had occurred over the past hundred years, and he showed what seemed to be an amazing ability to recall the essential details of each atrocious event.

Antagonism toward the fascist ideology being played out in the Spanish Civil War was an orientation Sol and Hyman clearly shared, and this could be reinforced by the fact that Hitler was an active supporter of General Franco, the Spanish fascist leader. German planes were being used to bomb towns in Spain still in the hands of the legitimate government. But there was too much negative interaction between my father and brother for them to realize that the daunting prospect of a common enemy could unify them.

While reflecting different times and cultures—Hyman a product of the Jewish experience in pre-revolutionary Russia, and Sol already thoroughly Americanized—my father and brother shared personality attributes that gave their political arguments an especially hard edge. Hyman could be merciless when he enunciated his political formulations, and he showed delight in exposing contradictions in anyone who might challenge his ideas. He was not averse to using offensive ridicule. In similar fashion, Sol had the skill to appraise the logic of an argument and could deftly point up inconsistencies as if he were a brain surgeon carrying out a difficult operation. His debating skills were honed in the sharp polemics in which he participated in left-wing gatherings in college.

As a thirteen-year-old with little experience in these matters, I found the political discussions between my father and brother confusing and sometimes scary to watch. I found the political cacophony surrounding me in my home highly embarrassing, and I often thought my family was weird. I had the impression that it was only in the context of the Fanshel family that politics took on the aura of a military battlefield.

It surprised me one day when I heard my father's defense of his attitude. His formulation took the following form: "If my child thinks differently from me on very important matters of politics, especially the fate of our Jewish people in this world, how can he love me?" That he should mention the word *love* was a singular event in my experience—it seemed to me that Jewish men of his generation rarely expressed affection openly—and this hit a receptive chord within my psyche. Hyman seemed particularly distressed that his firstborn son should turn against him in the important areas of ideology and ideas.

In rejoining the Fanshel family household, Sol felt compelled to turn over much of his paycheck to my mother and was thus deprived of the opportunity to enjoy the liberating rewards of working. He was genuinely concerned about the ordeal the family was going through because of my father's illness, but he also struggled with the issue of determining an appropriate share of his earnings to give to my mother for household expenses. Working full-time, he now functioned in an adult world, needing income to clothe himself appropriately. And he was eager to participate in a social life with other liberated young adults with whom he came into contact.

I gathered from what I heard in the ongoing family discussions that there was some dispute between Sol and Mom about the amount of money required to run a home. I was reminded of my own resistance to my parents urging their sons to contribute to the purchase of a new roll-away bed for my younger sister. But from my youthful perspective, I did not want my brother to make waves by challenging the arrangements the adults had set before him. I was a stickler for order, in a self-centered way, because this provided a more secure environment for me. Young as I was, I wanted a predictable life and was not sympathetic when I witnessed Sol challenging the way my mother calculated the financial needs of the family. Only chaos could come from such behavior.

In the ensuing years, when I would think of the experience our family went through, a sadness would come over me. It was not a happy time.

Cacophony, 1937

My father and brother are sparring
Tossing acrimonious words.
Each with a dagger to pierce the heart
Not in a fun mode on an athletic field.
Thrust poised to hit the target
Penetrating the other's defenses.
Cause pain.
Mesmerize.

Pop introduces the word.
He speaks of L-O-V-E.
A warming attachment
Between parent and child
And husband and wife.
Rarely heard in this household.
I cannot believe he said it.

My father proceeds to unravel
An engrossing conundrum.
He intones the challenging question:
"How can my son L-O-V-E me
When he does not think like me
About the fate of our people?"

Hyman recalls a humiliation
When arrested in years past.
Bolsheviks on the rise.
Caught twirling a cane on a corner
Selling coal to the highest bidder.
Still tasting the acidic gall.

The Firstborn Son Returns

And the son eight years my senior,
Dismisses with radical flair.
Should one receive greater warmth
In the chill of winter because
He has more dough-re-mi?
"Equal distribution to all" I say.
And the Talmud surely confirms,
Fairness and righteousness
Is what it is all about…

And I, in turn, the youngest male in line,
Present a query for your attention:
Dear Pa Pa and devoted brother.
How can I L-O-V-E you
When your raising me to live in fear
Compels me to recoil from both of you?

The violence of your convictions
And the noise of your chatter
Deliver the same sharp message:
Think like me or no L-O-V-E.
The words convey the danger…
Not to life, but to my soul.

The Author's Brother Jack Fanshel

7

Caught in the Squeeze

As my father slowly recovered from his heart attack in the waning days of 1936, we learned from our family physician that Pop could no longer negotiate the five flights of stairs to our apartment. Aside from our concern for his personal well-being, my father's being laid up and unable to work for the next six months also had the consequence that our family was no longer able to afford the rent we had been paying. The need to move dampened our spirits because we liked our present apartment, located in an attractive red brick building just off the Grand Concourse. Living in proximity to this upscale Bronx boulevard had given us a sense of status probably not warranted by our financial circumstances.

Mom quickly moved into action and found a cheaper rental on East 194th Street, just two blocks away. We were pleased that Pop would only have to negotiate a single flight of stairs, and that we younger Fanshels would not have to change schools.

But as we talked about our pending move, I could see evidence that Mom had been crying, and I understood that the change in our living arrangements felt like a comedown to her. She had always taken pride in maintaining a well-run and presentable household. We would now reside in a somewhat scruffy building whose exterior walls had been blackened by the passage of time. Having three strong Fanshel boys was a priceless asset when hiring a commercial mover was not within our means. After spending several days packing our dishes and other household items in crates and cardboard boxes, we loaded our belongings onto my father's Brockway truck to be driven by a friend to our new residence.

We offspring did not care as much as Mom did about appearances, but we nevertheless found the new apartment's smaller size confining. I discovered that personal space in which I could gather my thoughts was at a premium, and this made me fidgety. I felt as if I was always on public display, and the only way to become comfortable was to retreat into myself or to join my friends out in the street.

My propensity for turning inward was exposed at the dinner table one evening when my father directed a question at me which I failed to answer for several minutes. When I made a comment that was unrelated to the question asked, it was apparent to my family that I had been lost in my dream world. My weird behavior provoked laughter, and this was embarrassing.

The pattern of creating personal zones of privacy by closing myself off from the family likely accounted for my being out of the loop when Jack went through an important transitional life event. He became the focus of our family's attention when he revealed that he planned to drop out of high school and obtain a full-time job. He saw the family's financial difficulties and had decided that he might as well go out and get a job. He took on the heroic role of rescuing our family, with the declaration, "Somebody has to do something, and it might as well be me." Even though he was the sibling closest to me in age, I did not have the foggiest notion about what was going on with him, and I felt mortified that physical proximity had not led to more sharing and intimacy between us.

While detached from Jack, as from other members of the family, I was not emotionally removed from the catastrophe that had struck our household. The damaging reverberations from Pop's heart attack were ongoing for each of us and were like the outpouring of a water-main break. It was the most threatening thing that had happened to our family since the Fanshels arrived at

Ellis Island in 1920 without livelihood, money, or a place to stay. Our current situation was reduced to a simple reality: The flow of income made possible by my father's work had come to a halt.

Hyman's being self-employed meant there was no employer on the scene during this emergency who could be prevailed upon to help maintain our family until he recovered. Rent and utility bills had to be paid monthly, food must be purchased, and doctor's bills could not be ignored forever. Even the portion of Sol's wages donated to the family could not cover the expenses of our large household.

Prior to Pop's heart attack, Jack was able to take care of his own desire for spending money by securing part-time employment. For two days on the weekends in the spring and most of the week during the summer vacation, he worked selling hot dogs, candy, and ice cream for H.M. Stevens at baseball games at the Yankee Stadium or at the Polo Grounds. Grown men and older teenagers competing for these jobs turned out daily to apply for work at a lineup similar to that for stevedores at the docks. My brother invariably would get picked, because he was brawny and looked older than his years. When he came home from a ballgame, he would share his earnings with Mom, emptying his bulging pockets of the tips he had received. Knowing of his generosity, I was puzzled why Jack felt he had to contribute even more than he already was.

Within a week, Jack followed through on his announced intention and terminated his school career in his third year of high school. He succeeded in getting a job as a shipping clerk with a wholesale company that produced synthetic leather products used in the manufacture of furniture. While the work was boring and would likely do nothing for his development of a meaningful occupation, it did provide income to ease the family's strapped financial situation. I asked myself why it was up to Jack to rescue us.

I thought about my relationship with Jack and felt bad about being out of the loop when his decision to quit school was made. Ever since Ruth's birth when I was four displaced me from an improvised child's bed, Jack and I had shared the same double bed. I figured our closeness in age, only eighteen months apart, and physical proximity must count for something. Why had no family discussion about what was going on with Jack included me?

Within the limited housing space available for the six of us in our new living quarters, the determination of sleeping arrangements allowed little room for maneuver. My parents had the master bedroom to themselves, Ruth slept on the couch in the living room, and we boys were quartered in the second bedroom. The boys' bedroom had no closet, and there was one small bureau for the storage of clothes. Most of our daily wear hung on nails hammered into the back of the door. An assortment of pajamas, shirts, underwear, pants, and sweaters somehow remained suspended. In the midst of the clutter, a long salami was sometimes indecorously suspended on a hook screwed into the wall near the door. Salami and other smoked meats were often generously provided by our cousin Louis Feinstein, the delicatessen wholesaler in the family. We observed the rule: If you are home alone and Mom is not available to feed you, cut yourself a thick slice of salami and it will get you through the hunger pangs.

Our bedroom had two beds, with Sol having his own while Jack and I shared one. Jack was so large compared to me that the only way I managed to sleep with someone so massive and unmovable was to roll up into a tight ball and tuck myself in the corner out of harm's way. Later in life, when friends asked how my having to share sleeping arrangements with my brother for so many years had influenced my life adjustment, I let my eyes blink, affected a severe tic, and stuttered, "N-n-nothing at-t-t a-l-l. Can't you see I'm perfectly n-n-normal?"

Jack towered over me like a gigantic Adonis. Most of the time, he was good-natured and we got along satisfactorily as we grew up. Given the lack of space in our apartment, we tacitly understood that friction was best moderated by a pattern of avoidance. There were moments, however, when normal irritations could not be restrained, and Jack could not resist flexing his muscles in order to boss me around. When he indulged himself in this manner, it offended me and I would cook up a head of steam. Things got settled one day when Jack, stretched out on the couch reading the sports page, issued an order in the imperious tone of a general talking to his orderly: "Dave, throw this peach pit in the garbage can for me." I refused to obey his humiliating command, and I rebuffed him with a resounding: "To hell with you! I am not your slave."

A physical encounter followed, and it looked like Jack was going to make hash out of me. But he happened to be sunburned from having recently been at the beach, and his skin was as red as a boiled lobster shell. In the heat of our grappling with each other, I succeeded in stripping ribbons of skin off my brother's back with my fingernails. Jack's screams of pain followed me as I scooted out of the apartment. Later, my mother learned from Mrs. Weinreich, our next-door neighbor, that the Fanshel boys had been fighting "like hoodlums" in the apartment. Anything that turned out to be a "shame to the neighbors" was taboo in our family, and we caught hell for this violation of proper decorum. Despite this, it felt good to have overcome the tyranny of Jack's brotherly domination.

Jack also used his physical assets in more positive ways. He was a natural-born athlete. Aside from being tall and muscular, he moved with an unaffected grace. He participated in basketball at Schiff Center with guys who were accomplished players, and he held his own with the best of them. Aside from showing great speed, he managed to evade opponents in spectacular fashion by skillfully bobbing and weaving, and was able to score difficult basket shots repeatedly. When he collided with opposing players, his body mass earned him respect.

Jack's attachment to basketball motivated him to spend many hours in the local school yard practicing his jump shots and participating in games with pickup teams. He often returned home pouring sweat after running in the hot sun all afternoon. We would quarrel because he left his soggy sneakers to ripen under our bed, and the fetid odor quickly permeated our bedroom. The situation was resolved by our mother with the edict that the offending sneakers were henceforth to be placed outside on the fire escape for airing.

Exploiting his athletic skills enabled Jack to hang out with an older crowd. Most of these fellows lived in the West Bronx, and included in their ranks were budding actors, would-be boxers, and sophisticated types who dressed well and attracted good-looking girls. Jack enjoyed his acceptance among them and was impressed by the self-confidence with which his friends approached the world, the availability of spending money, and their seeming freedom from family constraints. Because he was immersed in this social scene, going to school was not a high priority for my brother, who was exposed to a model of young men who were growing into manhood in a hurry. Because he had the physique of a man, and a good-looking one at that, Jack developed a worldliness that may have set him on a fast track in life.

In time, I learned from Jack some of what prompted him to quit high school. Our first discussion took place one evening when we were alone in the kitchen. Mom had gone off with Ruthie to a special event at Schiff Center and had left our supper on the kitchen table. Pop, still recovering, was resting in bed. As usual, Sol was out and probably wouldn't come home until midnight. It was one of those rare occasions when Jack and I could have an intimate conversation.

I asked Jack about his decision to pull out of high school some months before. I probed the subject hesitantly: "You really surprised me."

"About what?"

"When you threw school aside. I can't figure out why you would want to do something like that. What got into you?"

He was silent for awhile, and I saw I had intruded into a painful area. He then whispered hoarsely, "He threatened her with a knife. I thought he was going to stab her."

"Threatened who? Mom?"

"Yeah. They were arguing about money. Mom said she was having trouble taking care of the family with the little money that was coming in. And Pop got all excited saying she was jumping on his back. As if he could do anything about it. They began shouting back and forth, calling each other names, and I heard her say some pretty nasty things about his always complaining about working, even when he was well. She got under his skin. And then it got quiet and I heard her say. 'Chaim, you're crazy. Put it down!' "

"And then what happened?"

"When I ran into the kitchen, he had a knife in his hand. When he saw me, he put it away and left. Mom was pale and had a frightened look but she wouldn't talk to me about it. I guess she was embarrassed because it was an ugly scene. Pop seemed like he really could do something to her."

The story was beyond my understanding because it did not square with my experience in the family. I had seen a great deal of verbal sparks flying between my parents, but nothing of a physical nature. I shared my confusion with Jack. "I don't understand this. To tell you the truth, I've never seen Pop pick up a knife or threaten her with his fists. I never saw him hit her."

Jack nodded. "Me neither. I never saw anything like this before. It shook me up. As I see it, things are falling apart in our family. This money business is making Pop go nuts. That's why I need to go to work and help out. I'm afraid he could kill her in one of their arguments."

I still could not conceive of my father physically harming my mother. It was too far out. Whatever his faults, he was not *that* kind of a man. He cared a lot about what people thought of him, and if there was anything important to Hyman, it was his dignity. He wanted people to think of him as a civilized man, an educated person.

What did ring true for me, however, was the picture of repressed rage Pop showed when people crossed or provoked him. I had sometimes experienced this quality in my own encounters, even though I did not pose a major problem for him. When incidents occurred and I recognized that he was seething inside, I tended to back off from disturbing him further.

I did recall, however, a recent experience when I happened to be alone in the apartment with my parents. I was taking a bath and heard my parents arguing in the kitchen. It was about money, of course. And my mother had a way of whiplashing Hyman with words. The fury of the verbal assaults heaped upon each other would build in intensity until Pop let go. Suddenly I heard him screaming at the top of his lungs, smashing dishes against the wall, one by one, with splintering sounds. The effect upon me was galvanizing. It reminded me of the time I witnessed a gang of tough kids throwing rocks at a glass conservatory. BAM! CRASH! WHOOPF! I sat shivering in the bathtub. No doubt about it, my father was going berserk. What I heard was disturbing to me, and the memory of the experience lingered with me for days afterwards.

Jack told me about another grievance with our father, one that helped seal his decision to give up his education.

"He *hurt* me," he whispered vehemently.

"How did he hurt you?"

This confirmed what we all knew. Our father's churlish behavior demonstrated that he did not understand the phenomenon of sports, even hated it, and he was opposed to any involvement of his children in organized athletic activity. His attitude made it clear that his early life in Russia was devoid of any exposure to sporting events.

Hyman often commented that he considered sports activity to be lowbrow and frivolous, not becoming to Jews. It was for the *goyim* (gentiles). He uttered the classic sarcastic comment of Jewish parents to straying sons: "What do you want to be when you become a man? A truck driver?" As mimicked by Jack, the words *t-r-u-c-k d-r-i-v-e-r* are drawn out for maximum effect. Ironically, the belittling delivery of the words gives a hint of Hyman's deflated self-esteem at having spent years in America driving his Brockway truck.

Jack related an additional exasperating habit of our father reflecting his antagonism to sports. Whenever Pop caught Jack listening to a radio broadcast of a football or a baseball game, he tossed a caustic comment in *ex cathedra* fashion: "*Voxt a bum dorten*" ("We've got a bum growing up here") and summarily turned off the radio. "That's my radio, for me to listen to," he would say. "You don't pay anything toward the rent or the electric bills. Why should you listen to the radio?"

Hyman also showed his disapproval when Jack played popular music on the radio. My father saw himself as the arbiter of musical tastes in the family. He had a devotion to grand opera and often repeated stories about his enjoyable visits as a young man to the world-famous Odessa Opera House. When Jack listened to the bands of Tommy Dorsey or Benny Goodman, the music was put down as vulgar, a *pista zach* ("common thing").

My father's dedication to operatic music indeed carried a high intensity. A story circulated in the family, repeated often enough to be believed, that when Hyman sold fruits and vegetables from a horse and wagon, shortly after the family arrived in the United States, he would sometimes quit work on Saturdays to attend the Metropolitan Opera. Purchasing the cheapest ticket, he would stand in the rear of the hall. Not knowing about American customs, he one day parked the animal and the attached wagon curbside, allowing this source of his livelihood to remain unattended for hours. A policeman came upon the scene and was provoked because the horse was being neglected and taxis were prevented from pulling up to the curb. When my father came out of the opera hall, the policeman gave him a dressing down and handed him a summons for obstructing traffic. But Hyman seemed proud of the violations ticket, since it constituted proof of his superior cultural commitments.

Jack's dramatic action in ending his school career was not an unusual occurrence in our Bronx neighborhood. Fueled by the economic depression that darkened the American atmosphere, there was an increase of incidents reflecting the degradation of personal decision-making, particularly evidenced among teen-aged boys. For example, Marty, who was well known to us, went off on a tear and wracked our neighborhood with gossip. He was the seventeen-year-old son of the Leibgold family, proprietors of a grocery store within a large food market around the corner from our house. One day Mr. Leibgold gave his son the day's cash earnings to deposit in the bank. However, Marty failed to return and his whereabouts were unknown. After several hours, the police were informed that Marty had disappeared and detectives were assigned to the case. The mystery was solved in a matter of days with the shocking revelation that Marty had run away with the cash that was entrusted to him. We later learned that the errant son had hopped a train to Florida, where he was involved in a spending spree when apprehended.

The neighborhood was alive with talk of Marty's venture into delinquency for days afterward. People were astonished by the moral depravity that motivated a child to steal from his own family. The self-centeredness of it all staggered the imagination, and concern was expressed about what was happening to the children.

My mother commented to Mrs. Weinreich, our *nexdoorika*, that she could not comprehend what she had heard: "A *Jewish* boy does something like this? Unbelievable!"

The story stimulated my interest and I was drawn to its details. I allowed my fantasies to run freely, and vividly imagined what it would be like if I were to engage in a similar disappearing act, taking off with Pop's bag of money while he was sleeping. I was intrigued that life offered such possibilities for transforming one's options in the world. I enjoyed picturing myself on a spending spree like Marty's, behaving with outrageous self-indulgence, including going to all of the movies I want to see, buying huge quantities of candy and ice cream, and even buying an expensive bicycle. But, alas, in my dream-like fantasy Marty's fate was repeated, and I suffered a denouement in which I had to face my parents when the police dragged me home. The shame created by my imagined exposure was so real that my fantasies extended to committing suicide. It was a relief to come out of my scary reverie.

Over the years, there has been speculation within the family about what Jack's life course might have been if permission had been given by our parents for him to play on the high school basketball team. Everyone who had watched my brother participate in sports had given him rave notices. If offered the chance, he would very likely have excelled as an athlete. An environment could have been created allowing Jack to enjoy the fruits of his talent and become a popular figure among the students. He surely would have been motivated to continue his schooling.

In conversations among the Fanshel children, the reproach for frustrating Jack's aspirations was directed at our father. My mother let Pop take the lead in this matter and never identified with any point of view, pro or con. She apparently had no knowledge of, or investment in, the subject of sports. Perhaps it was a matter of priorities, and she had other contentious issues to take up with our father.

Jack often expressed the view to me that our father's dictatorial control was a powerful negative influence upon his life that had particularly affected him. If Hyman had not demanded absolute adherence to his views, my brother would have had more opportunities to exploit his natural talents. And the coercive pressures were reinforced by the miserable economic conditions of the times we were living in. No question about it, Jack was caught in the squeeze of forces outside of his control.

Yet while these adverse influences were undeniable, I also see my brother's decision to leave school as a reflection of a self-generating force within himself, an assertion of his premature movement into manhood. Going to work in order to make right what was wrong with our family was, from his perspective, a manly thing to do. A kid's thinking, such as governed my own behavior, did not conceive of such a step as even remotely possible. Unlike Jack, I was not a man physically and was certainly not manly in my head.

Jack conceived of himself as a man because he had the physical attributes of a well-developed adult male. Hanging out with guys who were three or more years older also influenced him. They all supported themselves, and a number had left school early to get jobs. The times we were living in did not dictate that everybody should go to college.

Jack's friends had money in their pockets. They went out with girls who were women, with mature breasts provocatively displayed, and cosmetics and perfume liberally applied. More important, these guys were getting laid. They did not just talk about sex, as kids of my age were doing, they actually participated in the mating game.

My raunchy thoughts about what was going on in the lives of my brother and his friends were confirmed one summer evening. My parents and Ruthie were escaping the heat by staying in a modest rental cottage near Coney Island, and Jack and I were fending for ourselves in the city. I had a summer job delivering orders for a butcher, and Jack was working at his regular employment.

I came home late after hanging out in nearby Poe Park. My friends and I had spent the evening talking about our sexual fantasies after watching a married couple make love from the nearby roof of one of our group's apartment house. The man and woman had forgotten to pull down the shades, and much to their chagrin, they discovered their blunder only after they had concluded lovemaking. The voyeuristic impulses of teenagers prevented us from having any sympathy for the embarrassment felt by our luckless victims.

"Poe Park, a popular recreational area frequented by my friends and I, stretched two blocks on the Grand Concourse, the area's posh boulevard." (Photo by Percy Loomis Sperr, Milstein Division of United States History, Local History & Genealogy, The New York Public Library, Astor, Lenox and Tilden Foundations).

It was late, and I went home ready for sleep. When I tried to enter our apartment, I was surprised to find that my key did not work, and I realized that the double lock has been secured from the inside. I rang the doorbell several times, and after awhile the door was unlocked and Jack presented himself in his underwear with tousled hair and bare feet. Displaying a sheepish grin on his face, he hissed at me that he had a girl inside. I was given my marching orders: "Get lost!" And as an afterthought, "And don't come back for an hour at least." He slammed the door in my face and bolted the locks. After a long pause, stunned by my brother's command tactics, I had no recourse but to retreat to Poe Park, where I was left to sit alone on a bench in the dark, feeling put upon and miserable.

I could feel my teeth chattering, but it was not because I was cold. Something was going on that made me shrivel up. It had to do with sex as an activity that is performed and not just talked about. I could not get over the realization that my brother was getting laid. Jealous and admiring at the same time, I told myself that Jack was a really audacious guy. Not only was he making love to a girl, but right in our own apartment. I bet he was even doing it in Mom and Pop's bed! I kept asking myself: *"Where did he get the* chutzpah *to do something like this?"*

It is not to downplay Hyman's personal shortcomings as a parent that I identify the internally generated pressures experienced by Jack. There was a life force stirring within my brother, a part of his makeup, which led to his emerging early in life as a guy who pushed the boundaries of what was possible. He was making choices about what were age-appropriate ways of conducting his life. He was not playing the role of hapless victim in his overall functioning.

In later years, I concluded that the fact of whether or not one goes to college need not stand as a crucial test for evaluating life outcomes. Despite his grievances against Hyman, Jack went on to live fully by negotiating a strong marriage, glorying in the forward march of his three children and their spouses, and counting his blessings in having six strapping grandsons. He never missed a day in a lifetime of employment, supporting his family through honest labor in sales activity.

Jack's irrepressible energy, his determination to exact the most from what his circumstances allowed, was also apparent in the approach to the house he eventually owned in Massapequa. The first thing that struck you was that the home was surrounded by startling and even outlandish splashes of color, emanating from plantings that he extravagantly had installed wherever the ground permitted flowers to grow. His gardening proclivities stood as a metaphor for his positive approach to life. It could be said of Jack, as a child in one of my studies said about her life experiences in foster care: "You plant many seeds, and they may not all take hold or grow right away, but a garden can then replace the solid ground."

Hyman and Clara Fanshel

8

Life Resumes

After six months of home confinement, Hyman was sufficiently recovered from his heart attack to consider resuming a work life. He was looking forward to being active again, since staying home was very boring for such a restless man. And continued financial help from my mother's family was not something that could be tolerated much longer; Hyman's sense of pride made it uncomfortable for him to be unemployed.

Again, it was the extended family support system that provided a creative solution to the problem. My uncle Irving Kratchman proposed that Hyman set up a fruit and vegetable stand in front of his store, the Fair Deal Dairy. It was located a few blocks from New York's famous theatre district, in an area of the city with the unsavory designation of "Hell's Kitchen."

My uncle was already using the space in front of his store for a display of burlap bags containing all kinds of beans and specialty canned foods. They were stacked on boxes on each side of the entrance to the store. The many Italian Americans and other ethnic groups living in the area were a source of customers for the specialty foods that could be purchased at stores like his on Ninth Avenue.

Giving my father space to sell vegetables, fruit, and other items, therefore, meant a reduction in the income my uncle would derive from outdoor sales. Moreover, an adjustment was likely required on a psychological level by both men when Hyman became engaged in his little business in front of the Fair Deal Dairy. I wondered how many men would be comfortable with a brother-in-law entering into a work setting where the two of them would have to share space and see each other about sixty hours a week?

Nevertheless, my father seemed to thrive at the Fair Deal Dairy. Each day, he would take public transportation to the wholesale markets to buy fruits and vegetables, selecting the best buys he could find. Sometimes he would wind up selling unexpected items because they were cheap. You might pass his stand one day and see a basket of rubber balls or a box of scissors being displayed amidst the fruits and vegetables.

I was able to witness the drama of my father and my uncle embarking on this generous enterprise, where a helping hand was extended to a relative who needed employment, because my uncle included me in the package deal. I was invited to become a part-time delivery boy for the store on Saturdays, holidays, and in the summer. Fourteen years old at the time, it was new for me to take the subway from the Bronx to my uncle's store in Manhattan, and it made me feel grown up.

The opportunity of getting out of my cloistered neighborhood expanded my universe. My exposure to Ninth Avenue allowed me to observe urban life in all its vibrancy, and this may have contributed to my later interest in the fields of sociology and social work.

As a delivery boy in Hell's Kitchen, I enhanced my status with my Bronx friends because of some of the surprising places my Uncle Irving sent me to deliver grocery orders. It was hard for me to believe that I was being given the assignment of delivering sacks of cracker meal to Minsky's Burlesque Theatre. I did not know much about burlesque except what I had learned in evening conversations on street corners with my friends. My understanding was that such places were like movie theatres except that the entertainment consisted of women prancing around naked for an audience of admiring men whose intense gazes and appreciative cheers and catcalls attested to this as the ultimate life experience. At first, I wondered why people were eating so much cracker meal in such a setting, but then I was informed that the food item I was delivering was not for eating. It was to be spread on the stage floor so that the artistic ladies would not slip as they danced and undressed on the stage. I learned this by talking to inspectors from the New York City Fire Department, who were assigned to insure that the theatre was safe and, coincidently, spent time ogling the girls from backstage. They welcomed me to join them and thus introduced me to the forbidden world of sexuality in a more participant way.

On another occasion, I delivered groceries to a building adjacent to famous theatres. I brought my food parcels to the designated apartment, where I observed six women and a man hanging around; he was in charge. I soon learned that this was where prostitutes and their pimps waited for their customers to telephone for services. As I walked past the women to deposit my food delivery in the kitchen, they gave me playful pinches on my cheeks and uttered salacious taunts suggesting I was a handsome guy. Blushing profusely, I escaped as quickly as I could. I found myself wondering what Mom would think of her brother sending me to such a place. But I was glad she did not have a clue, because I had great stories to tell my friends.

As a teenager, I had the experience of working for both of my Kratchman uncles as a delivery boy. For each of my uncles I committed a blunder in job performance that brought forth their wrath, and revealed a kind of vulnerability or ineptness in certain aspects of my functioning that led my father to call me the family's *stadrayter philosophe* ("mixed-up philosopher"). He was referring to the quality of dreaminess I exhibited when withdrawing from family conflicts.

One year, I spent Saturdays working in Uncle Sam's hand laundry. I speculated why I was given the assignment even though the two Kratchman sons, Jackie and Ozzy, were likely persons to carry the responsibility. Perhaps my uncle knew I needed spending money and this was his way of getting some cash into my hands. He could be generous in other ways, for example, supplying the Fanshel boys with nice shirts unclaimed at his laundry. I figured that perhaps Ozzie and Jackie had commitments in activities that made them unavailable.

One day, Uncle Sam instructed me to deliver a large package of pressed bed sheets and linen tablecloths to a Mrs. Einstein, who lived in a fancy elevator building a block away from the store. As he gave me the parcels, my uncle carefully instructed me: "Don't leave the laundry with Mrs. Einstein unless she first pays you the bill of twelve dollars that she owes me for this delivery and for the last one where the bill is outstanding. Do you get me? *No payment, no wash!*" I agreed to the instruction.

After I arrived at the building in which Mrs. Einstein lived, I took the elevator to her floor. When I rang the bell of her apartment, I could hear high heels clicking on the floor as she came to the door and, without opening it, asked who it was. I told her I was from the Alden Hand Laundry and was delivering her laundry. She opened the door, and I could see she was somewhat younger than my mother, her hair was twisted in curlers, and she had lots of lipstick and face powder on her face. She was wearing a robe decorated with Chinese dragon designs. She looked me over suspiciously, extended her hands, and said curtly: "You can give me my packages."

When she reached her hands out to receive the delivery, I remembered to withhold the packages and told her breathlessly: "My uncle said I should not give you the laundry until you paid the bill for this delivery and for the last one, which is not yet paid." Her face took on a frozen grimace I found quite intimidating, and she said, "Wait a minute while I telephone your uncle." She softly closed her front door and I could hear her going into the interior of her apartment.

In a few minutes, Mrs. Einstein came back with a cheery expression on her face and reported her success to me. "Your uncle told me it is okay for you to leave the packages. I will drop by the store to pay your uncle after I go to the bank this afternoon." When I did not respond immediately, she demanded in a surly manner: *"Give me my laundry!"* Her face was frozen in fury.

With my heart beating at a rapid pace, I abandoned my cool and decided she could not be lying to me. I reasoned that grown-ups did not lie to young persons like myself.

When I returned to my uncle's laundry, he was busy talking on the telephone, so I sat in the rear of the store and began reading a magazine. When my uncle finished his call, he spoke to me in a soft voice, "You can give me Mrs. Einstein's payment." My heart pounding, the words tumbled out of my mouth in an almost incoherent way, "Mrs. Einstein told me that you said it was okay to leave her laundry, and she would pay you after she went to the bank."

The transformation of my uncle's face as he understood my failure to follow his instructions was something to behold. His eyes seemed to be bulging out of their sockets, and his face became beet red. He was so choked up that he could not talk to me further. He marched to the exit from the store and was gone for fifteen minutes. I did not know whether he had headed for a confrontation with Mrs. Einstein and perhaps had tried to shame her for lying to a teenager like me. Or, I reasoned, maybe he just walked around the block to cool off.

A few days later, I was talking to my cousin, Jackie, about my experience with Mrs. Einstein, and the aftermath bringing on his father's frightening response. I commented that I had no experience telling an adult, a seemingly rich lady no less, that she was telling me a falsehood. But Jackie could not contain his laughter. "Normally, my father is a nice, gentle dad; wouldn't hurt a fly. But when someone crosses him or disobeys him—or does something real dumb—then watch out! It's not that he'll hit you—but oh, that look! When it happens to me I shrivel up." Jackie insisted that he would rather be hit with his father's belt than have to face "the *look*."

Years later as I reflect on this episode, I realize it suggests a quality of naivete in my makeup as an adolescent. I showed difficulty in dealing with some of the harsh realities of adult lack of honesty, as was true of Mrs. Einstein, and behavior suggestive of pending violence, projected by my uncle.

Uncle Irving, Owner of the Fair Deal Dairy

A different kind of incident took place in my Uncle Irving Kratchman's Fair Deal Dairy store, where I worked as a delivery boy. On slow days when my delivery services were not being employed, I would be called upon to restock empty shelves.

One summer day, Uncle Irving instructed me to restock bottles of CN because the shelf was almost empty. CN was a popular household disinfectant manufactured in Buffalo. Its active ingredient was something called chloro-naptholeum, a highly noxious-smelling agent, which probably accounts for my uncle's frequent warning not to allow a bottle to fall to the floor because if it should break the "store will stink to high heaven."

So I went to the storage room in the basement and took hold of a new box of CN. I opened the top of the box in the basement and proceeded up the stairs to the store. I lowered the carton to the floor near the shelf space assigned for the product. Just then, a famous baseball player came into the store and the clerk, Paul Portnoy (my uncle's brother-in-law, employed at the request of my Aunt Rose), excitedly pointed the celebrity out to me. I became so engrossed in the opportunity to see this star, whose picture appeared on baseball cards that came with chewing gum, that I picked up the carton by the protruding flaps on the top of the box. I had been cautioned several times to always carry cardboard boxes containing glass bottles with my hands under the bottom of the box to carry the load.

The reader no doubt can anticipate what happened next. When I raised the cardboard box from the floor to put on the seat of a chair, lifting it by the tabs instead of the bottom, the weight of the contents suddenly forced the bottom of the box to fly open. Before I could prevent the disaster, the CN bottles fell to the floor with the sound of shattering glass registering painfully on my eardrums. A more noteworthy source of dismay was provided by the overpowering odor of fugitive CN fluid flowing in all directions on the store's tile floors.

My uncle's reaction to the mishandling of the box of CN brought on a second exposure to the "Kratchman look." It was bloodcurdling to confront the wide-eyed fixed stare that came my way and left me with a burden of guilt. Before me was a man who had given generously to my family in so many ways, not the least being that he was a major source of the financial support that paid for boat passage for our family and other relatives to come to the United States. I had let him down in an awful way, and I was not able to forgive myself. I would not have blamed him if he had banished me from the store. But my Uncle Irving did not take this path. His compassion extended to persons like myself even when not deserved. Which only made me feel more guilty.

What do these two episodes suggest about the kind of child I was? Perhaps Pop was right, I really did have the hallmarks of a "dreamy philosopher."

While a liability in the world at large, at home this tendency of mine to retreat into myself allowed me to avoid the fractious interplay that would take place when my parents, siblings, and I were all assembled at mealtimes. My state of dreaminess provided me with a protective shield from the rancor that might erupt because I was not prepared to challenge my father, as Sol was prone to do. The eight-year difference in age between us allowed my older brother to be more fearless and take more risks that I could.

When I think back to the Fanshel household in which I grew up, we all seemed to operate in our own worlds. One explanation of the limited communication patterns in my family may be the fact that my parents and Sol had been residing in the United States for only three years when I was born, and Mom and Pop hardly spoke the English language. This alone could contribute to the potential isolation of one generation from the other. Our parents really did not know what was going on in our lives when we were not home, and they were quite removed from our school activities as we grew up. It was as if they didn't have interest in such talk, which might not be a fair comment. But I was rarely asked, "So what did you do in school today? Are there any subjects you particularly liked?" When I received a medal for my performance in mathematics in public school, I was commended by my parents for having brought this token home. But this was the only time they connected with the subject matter I was being taught. And for some reason, I found not much of an audience with my three siblings for this kind of discourse.

A consequence of this lack of communication among family members was that my apparent success as a researcher in my mature years, with a fair amount of publicity and awards about my work coming to the attention of my family, seemed a surprise to everybody. There were congratulatory expressions of warmth of feeling toward me on such occasions, but there were also strong signs of being caught unawares. "Where did all this come from?" seemed to be the repeated refrain.

Over time, the relationships within our family became more expressive and more affectionate. But that's another story.

Part Two: Participating in WWII

Dave Fanshel, High School Yearbook Photo, 1941

9

Into the Wild Blue Yonder

In the spring of 1941, I was winding up my high school career at De Witt Clinton High School in the Bronx. It was a heady time for me, because youthful recognition had come my way. I had been elected as president of the senior class and recently designated in the yearbook as the "most popular" member of the class. Looking back, I am amused by this positive regard from my classmates and wonder whether I was courting approval in some way. I recognize the pattern of deference in my interactions within my family that might have extended to my peers and defined me as easy to get along with. My friends appreciated the fact that at least they could usually get a word in edgewise.

Our class's senior prom, a memorable experience, was held in the showy roof garden of the Astor Hotel on West 44th Street in the heart of New York City's theatre district. The music for the celebration was provided by the renowned Tommy Dorsey swing band and featured such singers as rising star Frank Sinatra, and Jo Stafford and the Modernaires, as well as trumpet player Ziggy Elman, famous for his performance of

"And the Angels Sing." My date, Sylvia Lieberman, was the attractive daughter of a local grocery store proprietor in our Bronx neighborhood.

Years later, I learned that two nationally recognized celebrities were members of our class, Richard Avedon and James Baldwin, both active at the time as co-editors of the *Magpie*, our literary magazine. Upon graduation, Avedon was chosen as poet laureate of the New York City high schools and later gained fame as a photographer whose portraits filled the pages of leading magazines. An important novelist, Baldwin garnered acclaim for his writing as a social critic of treatment of blacks in America.

Awaiting my entrance into the freshman class at the City College of New York, I found summer employment at J. S. Krum Candies, a large candy and soda emporium located on the Grand Concourse, a major boulevard in the Bronx. The area served as the locale featured in the film *Marty*, written in 1955 by Paddy Chayefsky, also a Clinton High School graduate.

My job called for me to put in long hours as a "soda jerk" serving the customers who came from all over the borough for ice cream sodas, sundaes, and the other mouthwatering offerings. I soon became skilled and felt a bit of pride in being able to hold three ice cream sodas in one hand, swiftly filling orders coming my way. When my friends came in as customers, I gave them special treatment by piling the whipped cream high on their ice cream sundaes.

The summer heat drew a large crowd of customers seeking cool refreshments. Catering to them in this noisy, crowded atmosphere felt demeaning. I learned that when otherwise normal people are thirsty and compelled to wait in long lines, their manners degrade and they do not always speak respectfully to employees.

On one occasion, I was belittled by a gruff man who loudly commented to another, "These days, Krum's seems to hire slowpokes to work the counters." When he summarily demanded a hot fudge sundae with the obnoxious instruction, "And don't be stingy with the nuts!" and further baited me with a query, "And can't we get things moving around here?" I had had all I could take. Striking back at this would-be tormentor, I dropped two scoops of ice cream directly on the counter in front of him, without the presence of a dish. I then poured gooey hot fudge over the gleaming stuff. While the customer stared at me wide-eyed, I slowly removed my apron and retreated to the cool basement of the store. This represents a most unusual display of temperament on my part, which occurs only when I am abused beyond tolerance. (When my family witnessed one of these odd moments, they used the label "quiet dynamite" to explain it.)

Six months after my graduation, the Japanese attack on Pearl Harbor took place on December 7, 1941. Within a day, President Roosevelt declared war on Japan, and with Germany shortly afterwards. Eighteen years old at the time, I was living at home with my parents and siblings, Jack, now 20, and Ruth, 14. Sol, 26 years old and a graduate engineer, lived with his wife in New York City.

All three Fanshel sons were subject to the military draft and would be in uniform within the first year of the country's entry into war. In 1942, Jack was assigned to the Army Air Corps as a technician, and was eventually sent with an air unit to the Pacific, serving in a headquarters company in a clerk/administrative capacity. Although not a combat soldier, Jack was involved in a major accident when a jeep in which he was riding in Okinawa overturned, severely injuring his back.

Sol entered the service in late 1942 as an engineering professional in ordnance research at the Aberdeen Proving Grounds in Maryland. His daughter, Susan, was born while he was in the service. Sol was able to commute periodically to the Bronx to spend time with his wife and child.

A student at the City College of New York, I chose to join the Army Air Corps Reserves, for which I would be trained in one of the flying specialties: pilot, navigator, or bombardier. Although joining this branch of service was a momentous decision on my part, I am not clear about what motivated me to enlist in a service where I would eventually be exposed to hazardous combat missions.

I was informed that there would be a delay in my being called to active duty until the availability of training facilities could be developed. In the meantime, as a preliminary requirement, I was obliged to report for a physical examination to the Whitehall Building in downtown New York City, a setting already famous as the entry point for military service for New Yorkers. I found the atmosphere dehumanizing, as we were herded around like cattle. I was ordered to strip naked with hundreds of other men while physicians examined the orifices of my body. I also underwent minute inspections of my genitalia and my behind. It was clear that personal privacy had become a thing of the past. The thorough medical inspection established that I was a healthy specimen, suitable for military service.

After about six months, during which I continued my college studies, I was called up for service in January 1943, and instructed to report for basic training in Atlantic City, New Jersey. This seaside resort had a long history as a high-priced recreational setting appealing mainly to middle-class vacationers. It was certainly more stylish than Coney Island, where I had spent many summers with my family in modest rental quarters.

No longer a recreational resort, the setting was now devoted to the Army Air Corps training operations. The posh hotels had been taken over to house the thousands of men destined to become pilots, navigators, and bombardiers. I was one of many recruits scheduled to spend six weeks in Atlantic City, transforming ourselves into soldiers. We were expected to learn the fundamentals of military life, such as how to march, salute, maintain the neatness of our persons and uniforms, and obey the rules. We would also engage in a strenuous physical exercise regimen to insure our being well conditioned and capable of coping with the vicissitudes of war.

It seemed that a major goal of the training program was to rid us of the notion that there was any area of our lives remaining under our own control. We were to think and act in the manner our superiors dictated. Every opportunity to drive home this particular way of doing things was exploited. One incident in particular reveals the process.

We had been training for two weeks without a break. Each day we were awakened at 5 A.M., herded around on drill fields, and engaged in many other activities until bedtime at 8 P.M. In order to condition us for sudden emergencies, we were sometimes arbitrarily awakened at 2 A.M. and assembled in front of our hotel to hear a lecture about discipline.

At the end of two weeks, we were informed that we would be allowed the coming Saturday as a day off for recreation and permitted to have visits from our families. There was the proviso, however, that we pass inspection on Saturday morning. Anxious to enjoy a day off with family members, ten of us assigned to a common suite of rooms at the Lafayette Hotel washed and polished our quarters most of Friday evening. By the time we were through, our rooms sparkled with cleanliness.

We were standing stiffly at attention as the four inspecting officers grimly strode into our suite that Saturday morning. I was so rigid I could hardly breathe. We watched as our visiting inspectors wiped every object and randomly selected furniture surfaces with their white gloves, checking for dust. They squinted at their gloves, and we felt elated that the inspection revealed no untidiness. My feelings of relief were extinguished in a moment, however, when a captain came hurrying out of the bathroom and reported finding a "disgusting" condition: unmistakable signs of a urine stain on the porcelain toilet. Someone had pissed with poor aim and had not wiped up after himself. Our day of recreation was canceled, and we were ordered to spend the rest of the day marching at Brigantine Field, where parades took place.

After the officers left, we stared intently at the toilet but could not discern any offending evidence of sloppiness. Nevertheless, I can attest to the fact that the Army approach to inculcating discipline works. For the rest of my life, I have never left a bathroom without inspecting the porcelain rim of the toilet for telltale signs of carelessness.

My parents visited me in Atlantic City a week later, after a bus ride of almost three hours' duration. Spending the day together in this setting was an adventure for the three of us. As with other immigrants to America struggling to survive, family and work responsibilities had kept Hyman and Clara Fanshel close to home, and they had not yet traveled much in their adopted country. Further, they were visiting me in a very unfamiliar military environment they could neither understand nor enter into comfortably.

The underlying emotions associated with our visit were obvious, since a nineteen-year-old son going off to war is a life event laden with deep feelings. We were undergoing a separation process, which was novel for my parents as well as for me. A year earlier, I had announced that I wished to go to the University of Michigan because I thought it would be more fun than staying at home attending City College. My mother was horrified, and her tears flowed freely at the prospect. With military service looming, I did not again discuss the idea of my leaving home, and the issue was never joined. Now the United States Army had transformed my status into that of an independent adult in the family.

My parents and I had a pleasant time together. Having been exposed to the cheerless environment of basic training, I appreciated the opportunity to receive my parents' full attention and affection. We decided to eat out at a restaurant, not a common experience during my growing up in the Fanshel family; such luxury had normally been unaffordable.

My father made a scene about our having to wait in line for a table. Adhering to the norms of queuing was not one of his social skills. I found their visit a warming occasion anyway.

In later life, I realized that I tended not to be aware of the vulnerability of my parents during my years growing up at home. I can now be more insightful about their emotional reactions to the fact that their youngest son was taking a path that might have dangerous consequences for his survival. From my own experience as a parent, I doubt that I could have handled their fears for my safety as stoically as they did.

After training in Atlantic City, I became one of a group of about one hundred aviation cadets sent to a college training detachment, a new type of training facility developed by the Army Air Corps. The program was housed within St. Vincent's College, a Roman Catholic seminary in Latrobe, Pennsylvania, some thirty miles from Pittsburgh. The seminary served under the auspices of the St. Vincent's religious order, and its main function was to train future priests.

Clara and Hyman Fanshel Visit David at Military Station in Atlantic City, New Jersey, January 1943.

The plan was for us to continue our basic military training and to take a variety of science courses relevant to aviation. Our qualified instructors were priests belonging to the religious order. A factor in the government's choice of the setting was the nearby availability of a private flying school, where we would be introduced to the phenomenon of flying and undergo the prescribed number of hours of flight training.

Within days of our arrival, it became clear that the host staff at St. Vincent's was anxious to make us aviation cadets feel at home. They appeared to be warm and gracious people, yet my new surroundings took some getting used to, given the fact that I had been raised in a strongly Jewish family where Yiddish was an important language. In this unfamiliar territory, the insularity of the home in which I was raised was readily apparent.

In addition to being an educational institution, St. Vincent's also included agricultural activities within its extensive acreage. Brothers of the order, dressed in simple religious garb, grew and processed much of the food we ate in the communal dining hall. In addition, a variety of domestic services, similar to those usually found in hotels, was provided by nuns attired in traditional habits. I sensed their reticence to engage in verbal interaction with the cadets as they doled out food in the serving line. They did not meet our eyes and exchanged no small talk.

The seminary continued to function in its normal manner as a religious training center despite the presence of aviation cadets. Because the atmosphere was informal, the daily activities of the seminarians were visible to us, and opportunities were available for interaction between both groups. It appeared we were accorded special regard because it was understood that we were being trained for combat roles in the war.

Sometimes, cadets and seminarians engaged in athletics together and appeared to enjoy each other's company. Many of the seminarians were good softball players and no slouches in touch football games. Looking at the handsome young men in the ranks of the seminarians, and their apparent normalcy as human beings, we cadets speculated about how such young men could contemplate a life of celibacy as part of their vocational commitment.

The seminary provided me with a novel social experience, immersing me within the heart of Roman Catholic religious life. It broadened my perspectives about my place within the human stream beyond my cloistered growing up in the Bronx.

I related my experiences as a resident in this Roman Catholic educational facility in letters to my parents. One incident surprised them greatly. I recounted how some of the seminarians had come to me shortly after we settled into our campus quarters. They had learned of my Jewish background and thought I might be a resource for a study course they found difficult. They represented a group of students being schooled in the Old Testament and were exploring the Hebrew language as a way of gaining more understanding of an important source of Christian thinking.

The seminarians felt they had hit pay dirt when I told them of my having accumulated six years of study of the Hebrew language in a religious school and also studied the language for two years at De Witt Clinton High School. I agreed to coach the seminarians each evening, and found it amusing to contrast St. Vincent's as a milieu for studying Hebrew with the little Jewish *heder* on Morris Avenue in the Bronx where I was enrolled as a six-year-old student. I recalled that in this early setting, I often had my ear twisted by a bearded rabbi-teacher who tolerated no nonsense from me when I looked inattentive.

As their mentor in the Hebrew language, I got to know the seminary students more intimately than would otherwise have been possible. This enhanced my sense of comfort with non-Jews. My relationships with the Catholic kids in the middle-class section of the Bronx where I'd grown up had not been ideal. The majority of them were enrolled in a parochial school run by Our Lady of Refuge Church, located a few blocks from my home, while I and most of my friends were students in the nearby public school. We essentially were segregated by the arrangements for participation in sports, with Jewish adolescents going to their own local community centers and their Catholic contemporaries participating in organized sports offered by the Catholic Youth League. Informal interaction between the two groups was often hostile and involved pejorative name-calling and fistfights over turf and alleged insults. I had had my full share of animosity towards these *"goyim,"* and because they were good street fighters, I had taken my lumps on occasion.

The benefits of my experience at St. Vincent's helped shape my social views. Although I do not carry a religious orientation as part of my personal outlook, I do not regard Christianity as alien, and can see its derivative sources in Judaism. I came to understand that much of the striving for a moral base represents a joint venture of these two religious strains. As a professor of social work in my later career, I became friendly with leading professionals working in the Catholic Charities social service organizations in New York City and Brooklyn, which included within their ranks bishops, monsignors, and sisters of religious orders. I sometimes attempted to score points with them by commenting about my experience as a "former Hebrew teacher of Catholic seminarians."

To round out our stay in Pennsylvania, we cadets engaged in an activity that might be called "dates" with local young women of Latrobe. With their parents' permission, they volunteered as members of a female service organization to socialize with the military visitors. Two other cadets and I shared camaraderie with two sisters from a local family and one of their friends. We had a good time together within the limited recreational resources of Latrobe. The girls' families were Polish American and lived modestly. Their fathers and brothers were coal miners. When visiting in their homes, I was introduced to the use of the outhouse, since indoor plumbing was not available.

Although I was Jewish and the young women's families were Roman Catholic, I was treated with apparent easy acceptance. We cadets were invited to participate in Sunday dinners, where the food offerings reflected talented cooking skills and the atmosphere was lively. We were also invited to join the fathers and other adult male relatives at the headquarters of the Latrobe Literary Club, a cover title for an organization whose only purpose was conviviality. It provided opportunities for unrestrained drinking on the weekend in a state where bars were closed on Sundays.

One phenomenon that surprised me about my social experiences with the local men I met in Latrobe was the often expressed belief that there was a tunnel connecting the male college campus at St. Vincent's with the counterpart female institution, Seton Hill College, some five miles away in Greensboro. It was believed that the faculty priests met the faculty nuns for secret rendezvous. These reports of underground assignations sounded like excerpts from *The Canterbury Tales*.

I went out with the same pretty young woman on a number of occasions, and our relationship took on an aura of romance. Memories of this interlude would later become source material for sexy dreams during the dog days of flying combat missions from Italy. Luckily, this ecumenical social adventure was a time-limited experience, given that I would soon be shipped out to the next training station in the program. Who knows what complications would have arisen if a relationship involving young adults from such disparate backgrounds had continued?

Meanwhile, the flying lessons provided at the local airport were hardly pleasurable. I participated in ten hours of flight training with a barnstorming macho flying instructor who sought to impress me with the many acrobatic maneuvers he had mastered over five years of flying. Since I had never flown in an airplane before, being subjected to crazy loops, simulated stalls, and a variety of other sources of challenge in a two-seater training plane—often buffeted by winds—left me very queasy and unsettled. I suspected that the instructor knew full well that by his grandstanding behavior he was forcing me to deal with scary sensations. Perhaps he enjoyed putting in his place a cadet who might think of himself as a potential hero but who nevertheless was obviously still wet behind the ears.

The threat of being removed from the program because of chronic airsickness was real and made me tense. I was determined that I would not heave up my lunch. I knew I would have to work with all the self-control that I could bring to bear if I was going to become a "flyboy."

Dave Fanshel, "Flyboy"

There was a need for pilots, bombardiers, and navigators to man the tens of thousands of airplanes rapidly coming off the assembly lines of manufacturing plants in the United States. After concluding our stay at St. Vincent's, we were sent to a classification center in Nashville, Tennessee, where the aviation specialty to which we were best suited and in which we would be trained would be determined.

Soon after our arrival at the Nashville Center, we were subjected to many tests to measure natural and acquired skills relevant to the demands of the air war being waged by the United States. One of the intellectual leaders of the procedures developed to classify the cadets under the rubric of aviation psychology was John Flanagan, a psychologist on the faculty of the University of Pittsburgh. He had carried out interviews of aircrews coming back to their bases after bombing runs on enemy targets in Europe to determine what behaviors were called into play by the demands placed upon pilots, navigators, and bombardiers. He was interested in "critical incidents" taking place in the men's performance where their capacities for combat assignments might be measured.

A sense of the procedures we were required to execute can be provided by a few illustrations. For example, one task I faced as a subject involved my holding a metal prong for a period of time in the center of an electrified field bordered by a metal ring. I was required to avoid contact with the ring while being badgered by the tester with provocative verbal taunts. Presumably, this offered an objective measure of my ability to continue a task under stressful conditions. Another test required taking pegs out of a board, turning them around, and inserting them back in the board. The speed with which I was able to perform these operations was recorded and intended to simulate the task faced by bombardiers in fine-tuning the knobs of a Norden bombsight under combat conditions.

Many such tests, some of which struck me as quite clever, were administered over several days. Since the tests had been formulated on the basis of observing air personnel already known to be successful in the execution of real-life military assignments, it was assumed that the resulting scores would provide a valid prediction of the outcome of training efforts.

When the testing procedures were completed and analyzed, each cadet was given his performance scores in summary form before leaving Nashville. A perfect score would be 10. I thus learned that I had achieved the following results:

Pilot: 4
Navigator: 9
Bombardier: 8

The low score achieved in predicting my suitability for pilot training, while unflattering, came as no surprise. Since I had never driven a car before entry into military service, the responsibility for the control of a moving vehicle was a novel experience. Given this simple truth, I was taken aback when notified of my assignment to the group of cadets participating in the primary pilot training program at Maxwell Field, an airbase in the vicinity of Montgomery, Alabama. Training as a pilot required a sequence of three training settings at different Army Air Corps bases: primary, intermediate, and advanced.

The classification test data calculated about me clearly defined my potential as *least* promising for the category of pilot training. Through inquiry of training officers at Maxwell Field, I learned that there was an urgent need for pilots in the war effort. My test results were being ignored with an apparent willingness to take the risks of training failure.

From the moment of my entrance to the grounds of Maxwell Field, I was compelled to face the fact that I was in a place where no-nonsense martinets ruled the roost, and where the serious business of waging war dictated the content and form of all program activities. Each individual cadet had to shape up, and I quickly got the message.

A variety of academic courses were to be taken in classrooms, including aircraft identification (friendly and enemy), elementary navigation, aircraft mechanics, weaponry, and meteorology. Time investments were also made in standard military routines, such as marching on parade grounds, going on long hikes into areas of rough topography, and target practice. Most important, flying experience was to be obtained in training aircraft more powerful than the Aeronca planes and Piper Cubs I'd flown in when stationed in Pennsylvania.

We were quartered in permanent barracks, and our training time was tightly scheduled to maximize the goals specified at some upper level of Army Air Corps leadership in Washington, D.C. We were awakened early and our days were full. Recreation in the evening was at a minimum, and we went to bed in a state of physical exhaustion.

One day, we were taking part in a simulated forced march, requiring us to hike a considerable distance over a terrain known as the "Burma Road" obstacle course. Its notorious reputation was borne out as men kept collapsing from the effects of the heat. The sun beat down mercilessly, and the temperature rose to 100 degrees Fahrenheit. By the time we had completed the full-course run, I was unbearably hot, with body sensations I had never experienced before. It was almost as if I was about to faint.

When we were dismissed and directed to return to our barracks, my sense of being on fire was so powerful that I ran into the shower, fully clothed, shoes and all. Although I turned the water on full blast, I remained in a state of extreme distress and felt compelled to report to the medical service for assistance. It was determined that I had a temperature of 105 degrees, and I was ordered to lie in a bathtub loaded with ice until the danger of heat stroke was relieved.

Soon after this incident, the inspector general at the base alerted the commander of Maxwell Field about what was going on. More sensible rules for marches were promulgated to protect the health of the cadets from the zealousness of those in charge of the physical conditioning.

By design, events were also organized to modify civilian orientations that might undermine military discipline. An example of this occurred early in our training, when we were brusquely aroused from sleep at 3 A.M. and ordered to get into parade dress attire. We assembled at the central parade grounds despite being half-awake and confused about what was going on.

When we were in proper formation and called to attention, the booming voice of the cadet regimental commander announced in a stentorian cadence the purpose of our gathering: "Aviation Cadet Samuel Blair has been found guilty of cheating while taking an aircraft identification examination. He has brought dishonor on the Aviation Corps. He is a disgrace to his uniform. Samuel Blair is hereby stripped of his status as an aviation cadet. He is to be expelled from Maxwell Field forthwith and sent to an appropriate assignment for military duty. He is without honor, and his name is never to be mentioned again at Maxwell Field."

While we remained at attention, a forlorn figure emerged from the darkness, an aviation cadet whose movements in a stooped posture symbolized his disgrace. The insignia he wore was then torn from his uniform in violent gestures by the adjutant, and his barracks bag was tossed into a wheelbarrow. In our last sight of him, he pushed his load toward the railroad platform where he would board a train for parts unknown.

This theatrical display to which we had been exposed likely had its origins in the practices of the military academies at West Point and Annapolis. It was clearly designed to make a permanent impression, and the exercise in public humiliation had its intended impact upon us. The separation from civilian life was beginning to shape our psyches.

Scoring well on tests, however, was not my problem. A greater challenge was taking place at the large airfield nearby where hundreds of aviation cadets were having their first flights in training planes. Early on, the aim of instruction was to get each cadet past the milestone of flying his first solo flight.

As my flying instructor directed me to take the controls and I sped the plane down the runway for takeoff, it was impossible not to be distracted by the eruptions taking place in my stomach. Fighting queasiness, I zigged and zagged all over the place on takeoff. Once airborne, I performed adequately in straight and level flying, but the violence of my landing was pronounced, threatening the integrity of the aircraft's struts.

I was acutely aware that I was in danger of being "washed out" because of the uncertainty of my reactions to the physical phenomenon of flying. I found such an outcome unacceptable, since it would define me as a failure in the most important venture I had embarked upon in my life to date. The thought of it caused me great anguish. Nevertheless, I was compelled to face the reality that my motivation for joining the aviation cadets was not based upon any familiarity with the nature of the training assignment I would be undertaking.

Physically and conceptually, being upside down in space was an unfamiliar world to me, and the emetic effects were predictable. I also considered the fact that the classification test scores assigned me in Nashville were clearly prophetic and had provided no grounds for optimism that I had the makings of a pilot. My washing out would indicate that a score of 4 for pilot training, out of a maximum of 10, as contrasted with a 9 for navigation and 8 for bombardier, had been strongly predictive of my training outcome thus far.

I was also uneasy about the prospect that I would be deemed unfit for transfer to another flying assignment as a navigator or bombardier. My continued airsickness might lead to a decision by those in charge of the program that any assignment requiring flying experience would leave me so disabled as to be unable to function in any assigned tasks.

To deal with my dilemma, I came to an outlandish solution to my problem: I vowed that I would never vomit in the presence of my flight instructor. As anyone with personal experience in this realm knows, this is not an easy demand to make upon oneself. Yet, I somehow succeeded in my effort at self-control. Even when subjected to various acrobatic maneuvers carried out by my instructor, I successfully held back the urgent impulse to heave my guts out. Over a number of training flights, I showed no outer signs of the mammoth stresses taking place in my body, although on several occasions I came very close to powerfully disgorging the entire contents of my stomach.

Such goings-on exacted a price in my physical well-being: Taking a look in the mirror after a training flight I saw that I looked ashen.

This drama went on for about a week, and somehow I managed to maintain my resolve, despite my internal body workings emphatically protesting this form of self-abuse. I was reminded of the adage attributed to a Native American wise man: "Every man likes the smell of his own farts." To which I would make an exception: "Not if you have been swallowing your own puke for a week!"

The resolution to this nightmare came one day after a particularly horrific flying lesson. Takeoff and landing exercises had been hairy, and even the instructor was beginning to look a little green. After about a half hour of this sojourn in hell, he suggested that we have a conference in his office. When we were seated, he stared at me for a short while, his expression conveying a half-pitying and half-mocking attitude. He searched for words and finally uttered the fateful news. "Fanshel, I really do think you could learn to fly someday. You clearly have the brains, and you can learn. *But the war won't last that long!*"

Although not unexpected, absorbing the news was difficult. Being washed out of pilot training was an embarrassment, an assault upon my sense of self. I thought ahead to how painful it would be to tell family and friends that I was not good enough to be a pilot. However, I was relieved to learn within twenty-four hours that my instructor had decided to recommend that I continue in the training program for flight personnel, either as navigator or as bombardier. I sensed that he knew that I had been airsick on every flight we had taken together. The fact that I had not allowed myself to heave my guts had apparently earned his respect.

Looking back now at this episode in my life, I of course have a gentler view of the experience. I am inclined to say to my earlier incarnation: "David, we cannot be good at *everything*. As later developments proved, you are good at *something*. In your failure, you revealed a quality in yourself that may have been more important for survival in life than gaudy success in all undertakings." But of course, it is easier for the senior person to be understanding because he has the advantage of a known outcome. Disasters at a young age always leave the fear that a pattern of failure is unfolding, that one's future will always be compromised.

Decisions about my career as a would-be aviator were finally proceeding more rationally. When I left Maxwell Field, I was informed that I would be trained as a navigator. This made sense, as I had scored quite high in this area in the performance tests taken at the Nashville Classification Center. Although I did not know much about the new training assignment, I looked forward to the experience because it provided me with a new beginning after my ignominious experience as a pilot trainee.

Before entering the Navigation School at Selman Field in Monroe, Louisiana, I was sent for a three-week course in aerial gunnery. I traveled by train to Fort Meyers on the northeast coast of Florida. Here, I checked into Buckingham Field, where I was immediately involved in a continuous rote-learning experience designed to prepare me to function as a gunner on a heavy bomber aircraft such as a B-17 Flying Fortress or a B-24 Liberator, both powered by four engines. All aircrew members were required to be competent as aerial gunners, even though their primary assignments might be that of bombardier, navigator, or flight engineer. Crewmen whose responsibilities were concentrated solely upon aerial gunnery might be housed in turrets capable of rotation in the tail, nose, or underbelly of their planes or standing at their posts at the open waist windows at the sides. Gunners became the defenders of their aircraft when fighter planes of the German Luftwaffe attacked. We learned that bombers flew in tight formations in order to maximize their firepower against incoming enemy fighter aircraft. The gunner's function was clearly vital for the survival of the aircraft.

Since bomber planes were equipped with fifty-caliber machine guns, it was expected that we would get to know this piece of equipment as well as we knew our own bodies. We spent considerable time taking the weapon apart and putting it together again and finally were tested on our ability to perform this task blindfolded. I was pleasantly surprised when I demonstrated my competency in performing this task.

Much of this training focused upon learning to shoot accurately. We began with rifle practice in which shooting was directed at fixed targets at the firing range. We then advanced to shooting a rifle standing on the back of a truck as it traversed a circular track. Each time the truck ran over a trip wire, it released a skeet, a clay disc that sailed into the air in unpredictable directions. We learned to track the skeet in flight by tracing its path in a sweeping motion and accommodating to its speed; the trick was to fire at the right moment so as to strike it down. There were about twenty-five traps releasing skeet in one trip around the track. If one lost sight of the serious purpose of this training, it could be defined as a kind of fun-and-games activity suitable for carnivals.

Later in our training, we changed from ground-based activities to shooting at targets from various positions on trainer aircraft. A second plane towing a target sleeve extended on a rope provided us with a moving object to fire at. This experience more realistically simulated the combat conditions we were likely to encounter in the future. On these flights I became pleasantly aware of the fact that I was beginning to feel comfortable in the air and did not show any signs of the appalling airsickness previously experienced in pilot training. *Hallelujah!*

I left Florida with a sense of having acquired some beginning military skills.

There were several navigator training schools located in different areas of the country, and I was sent to one located in Monroe, Louisiana, a small city in the northern part of the state. Selman Field was a substantial air base that contained a fleet of planes used for training flights. They provided the opportunity for aviation cadets like myself to track the course of aircraft, to develop estimated times of arrival at destinations, and to use various modes of determining the directional headings pilots required for getting bombers to targets.

In the spring of 1944, there was a shortage of navigators to serve with flying crews sent on new heavy bomber planes to participate in the wars in Europe and Japan. There had been particularly heavy losses of American aircraft flying from England and Italy against German targets. The bombers were engaged in strategic bombing missions calculated to destroy factories producing German weapons of war such as aircraft, tanks, and munitions, as well as sources of fuel supplies and transportation systems required to bring these military necessities to German combat sites. In response, the German Luftwaffe had been engaging in a vigorous defense of their strategic assets, with hordes of fighter planes aggressively seeking to interdict flights of B-17's and B-24's. The enemy had been quite successful in shooting down many American and British planes, and the replacement of aircraft was given a top priority as necessary to winning the war.

Monroe, Louisiana, was in the middle of backwater country. It was racially segregated, and struck me, perhaps unfairly, as having a predominantly "redneck" population whose ideas seemed to stem from the Confederate experience in the Civil War. Hot and steamy, the town offered little to the aviation cadets in the way of recreation—except drinking and carousing—on rare days off. On the base, the military personnel and the civilian employees frequently revealed attitudes aligned with the Old South. Occasionally a whiff of anti-Semitism was discernable from the officers training us as well as from the civilians, but I was too taken up with my duties to pay much attention to such atmospherics.

I sailed through the navigation training and emerged as an officer ready to join a combat crew. Very curious about what lay ahead and wary of the dangers involved, I took my leave of Louisiana.

The Myakin' *Crew at Biggs Field, El Paso, Texas, May 1944:* Rear (left to right): *Mike Heryla, bombardier; Jim "Woody" Dunwoody, copilot; Jim McLain, pilot; Dave Fanshel, navigator.* Front (left to right): *Mario Caserta, flight engineer; Tommy Barr, ball turret gunner; Vern Polasky, tail turret gunner; Harold Lopeman, radio operator and waist gunner; Wayne Martin, waist gunner; (unknown, later replaced), nose gunner.*

10

Crossing the Atlantic

In the early spring of 1944, the ever-expanding incursions of American air bomber fleets into the German heartland had wreaked havoc with the enemy's capacity to engage in combat. Strategic targets such as aircraft manufacturing plants, petroleum-processing facilities, and ball-bearing works were being systematically destroyed in daytime bombing raids. But the destruction carried out by massive formations of B-17 and B-24 bombers did not come cheaply. A formidable massing of antiaircraft guns strategically distributed around the targets and a still-resilient and determined Luftwaffe succeeded in shooting many Allied bombers from the skies.

In order to compensate for the heavy losses of planes and their crews, military planners in Washington, D.C., assigned a high priority to the task of replenishing U.S. flight personnel. Because shortages among categories of trainees were unevenly distributed, replacement combat crews often were formed and prepared for overseas duty before the navigator positions could be filled. As a result, navigator trainees like myself were turned out on a hurry-up basis.

Recently commissioned as a flying officer, I arrived as a Johnny-come-lately at the crew training facility at Biggs Field outside of El Paso, Texas. This was the facility where men were assembled from the various Army Air Corps training schools around the country and allocated to the crews with whom they would fly in combat missions overseas. Once assigned, it was understood that from then on, the military careers of the ten men constituting a crew would be intertwined and that they would have to depend upon each other for the effectiveness of bombing raids upon the enemy as well as for personal survival.

Newly assigned to a crew formed about a month earlier, I found that my comrades had already had some solid experience in flying practice missions together. Under the leadership of Jim McLain, the commanding pilot, they were in the process of bonding as a group. While the men welcomed me in a formal way, I sensed from my interaction with them that judgments about the value of what I had to contribute to the common effort were suspended until I demonstrated performance capability on our practice flights. As an unknown quantity, I might emerge as a welcome addition. But I could also turn out to be a fuck-up capable of undermining the group's chances for survival. Time would tell.

With the ten of us originating from nine different states, our diversity as a crew was readily apparent. I recognized that there was a part of me that immediately felt different. Having spent my life largely immersed within a homogeneous Jewish population, I struggled to overcome the psychological self-restrictions of my childhood. I realized that I was now in the midst of greater America, where the Jews are a distinct minority. As I had earlier at the Seminary, I was forced to face the essential insularity of my family origins in the Bronx, where we lived in semi-hostile isolation from the next street populated largely by Roman Catholics.

In my growing up, my parents and their relatives and friends reinforced this sense of being separate from non-Jews, referring to *goyim* ("gentiles") as if they were a species apart. I wondered if my crewmates were going through a similar process of adjusting to an unfamiliar social situation, even though they were more like each other than like me. I was sensitive to the possibility that they might well look upon me, the only Jewish guy on the plane, as an exotic specimen.

Luckily, my concern with being accepted was transitory, and I quickly realized after a few training missions that there was only one task worth my concentration: to learn how to be effective in combat. As a navigator, I would be called upon to give guidance to our pilots about the plane's location when we were part of an organized bomber formation. If our plane were assigned to lead the group on a mission, my role would be significant in getting us to the assigned target on a course prescribed in the preflight briefing. If ever we were separated from the group, my job would be to guide us safely back to home base.

Along with the rest, I was soon involved in practice sessions where we focused upon sharpening the skills we would require. We simulated such combat flying routines as making rendezvous with varying numbers of planes from our group; advancing in tight bomber formations to targets designated for destruction; identifying aiming points for the bombardier; conducting special bomb runs at high altitudes; and returning safely to our air bases. The specialized roles assigned crew members had to be synchronized within and between planes in an intricate assortment of maneuvers and transactions.

We spent the six weeks following my arrival engaged in such realistic combat exercises, feigning defensive strategies to counterattacks that might be made against us by enemy aircraft and gun emplacements on the ground. In eager-beaver fashion, I invested myself in these training routines. We flew daytime cross-country missions as well as overnight practice trips, where I honed my skills in determining our position at any time by taking fixes on stars with my sextant.

At the end of the training experience at Biggs Field, I was pleased to find that I was able to successfully guide an airplane over long distances, managing to get us to our assigned destinations with an acceptable level of success. I also showed increasing accuracy in calculating estimated times of arrival (ETAs) at targets and other destinations.

As the training process continued, I was more securely finding my place as a member of the crew. The practice missions brought us together in working relationships in which I had the opportunity to demonstrate competence, and I was glad to note that my sense of being a stranger gradually dissipated. The intimate living situation helped remove whatever exotic peculiarity we ascribed to each other and initially responded to. We discovered that we were just people with common human needs, not radically different from the folks at home.

We crew members often speculated about what it would be like to fly missions against well-defended German targets. Our instructors, veterans of combat, told us that planes were being shot down all over the place and that the pilot played a key role in determining the outcomes of missions—whether the crew survived or was killed.

"If this is true," I thought, *"we have lucked out in Jim McLain."* My impression of Jim was positive: He was a strong personality and not someone who could be pushed around. Although not foolhardy in asserting himself, he seemed unlikely to be cowed by authority.

Jim cut a manly figure in his crushed flyboy's cap and in the easy grace of his walk. I was not surprised when I heard that he played varsity football at his high school in Louisville, Kentucky.

One side of Jim's family originated from Tennessee, where a grandfather had served with the Confederate States of America in the Civil War and wound up being held in a Yankee prison under harsh conditions. This would account for the residue of anger in the way Jim talked about this aspect of his family's history. I also learned that he had a twin brother at home.

Jim was not prone to grandstand, and he avoided unnecessary risks as the commander of our airplane. He had a quality of steadiness that would stand us in good stead. We soon learned that he could be tough and keep a tight rein over what went on in our crew's operations. Even at this early point in our relationship, I expected him to keep his cool and make sound judgments in dangerous situations.

Knowing that I was fresh out of navigator's school, without much experience under my belt, Jim went out of his way to be supportive. He offered kudos when my estimated times of arrival for reaching practice mission destinations proved accurate. I was pleased to be developing a good working relationship with him. This fact helped me face the reality that we would soon be participating in air combat missions where our survival as a crew would depend upon our working together in a coordinated way.

Two of our crew, Mike Heryla and Hal Lopeman, were married and lived with their wives in rented quarters near Biggs Field. Mike, our bombardier, had been married to Faye for several years. She was a petite and attractive woman, and I sensed that behind her soft-spoken, well-bred Southern manner lay a strong-willed and sophisticated personality. The couple's devotion to each other was readily apparent, and a pleasing atmosphere of ongoing romance seemed to emanate from them.

At age twenty-eight, Mike was one of the older men on our crew. A dark-haired, solid-looking man with even features and a ready smile, he shared the nose section of the B-24 with me and the gunner assigned to the nose turret. Mike had a working-class background and had spent part of his childhood in a coal-mining community in Pennsylvania. He had worked in the mines for several years with members of his family. I was impressed to learn that he played semi-pro baseball in his youth.

Mike was a somewhat quiet guy, not prone to run at the mouth. Although he had worked in New York City for a few years, he did not have the native New Yorker's speech dialect, as I did. He was not easily ruffled on our practice missions, and when we worked closely in the nose, often in crouched positions, I found things went smoothly for us. This, too, boded well, since we would have to work collaboratively in our mission tasks of identifying and hitting strategic targets with our bomb loads.

As bombardier, Mike would be called upon to arm the bombs we carried on our missions. Using the Norden bombsight to zero in on targets, it was his job to release the bomb loads according to briefing instructions. He had been trained to handle explosives, so if bombs got hung up in the bomb bay, as sometimes happened, he had the responsibility to disarm our volatile cargo. The procedure was delicate and hazardous and involved walking with a portable oxygen tank on the catwalk in the bomb bay in the subfreezing temperatures that often prevail at high altitudes. Since the task of disarming bombs requires manual dexterity in the manipulation of sensitive gadgetry, his having been a good athlete, I reasoned, might augur well for the way he would carry out his responsibilities.

Hal Lopeman functioned as our radio operator and would also be called upon to position himself as a waist gunner in the event that we were under attack. We would depend upon him to keep in communication with our air base and also to provide me with navigational fixes in our line of flight, based upon the radio beams he would be monitoring.

Hal and his family also had Midwestern roots. I found a quality of earnestness in the way he conducted himself both on practice missions and in other aspects of our lives in the military. A straight arrow, he tried to do everything right, which perhaps reflected his strong religious commitment.

There was another side to Hal, however, that diminished any sense of the do-gooder. He possessed a sense of humor that came out in gushes of youthful enthusiasm and playfulness.

Hal had only recently married Mabel, a vivacious and well-spoken young lady from his hometown. Our environment at Biggs Field struck me as a rather bleak setting for a honeymoon, but this reflected the reality of the war environment in which we were living. While I marveled at their decision to tie the nuptial knot, they obviously enjoyed being together. Even though Hal's survival in our approaching combat stint was chancy, at best, they made the most of the remaining few weeks they had before we left for overseas.

When the time came for our departure, the scene in which the two married couples in our midst took leave of each other was poignant. Yet, despite the obvious distress of separation they experienced, I felt envious of my crewmates in being involved in committed relationships. I would be strengthened, I thought, in facing the prospect of death in combat if my life were also rooted in an affectionate tie. The thought of possibly being killed in action evoked a morbid sense of loneliness.

The time for our direct involvement in the war had arrived. We departed Biggs Field in Texas and began our overseas journey to our European destination. As we left, we learned that the Allied D-Day invasion of Normandy had just taken place on June 6. The war against the Germans was now in full force, and we were about to be part of the historic effort.

We flew first to Wichita, Kansas, where a giant Consolidated Aircraft Corporation plant turned out B-24 Liberators in a vast assembly process. Equipped with four powerful Pratt & Whitney engines, the Liberator would be the most heavily produced American bomber of World War II.

We were assigned a sparkling new Liberator to carry us to an air base located in Europe. The bomber plane's aluminum covering glistened in the sun, an impressive product of American manufacture. We were only temporary guardians of this precious commodity, however—the delivery boys, so to speak. Once delivered, it would be flown by some other crew for immediate use in bombing strategic German military targets.

Our itinerary called for us to travel to Dow Field in Bangor, Maine, from which we would fly to Gander Lake in Newfoundland, Canada. It would then take us about 8½ hours to travel to Lagens, located among the Azores in the North Atlantic Ocean. The following day we would move on to Marrakech, Morocco, on the western coast of Africa. We would then head for Algiers, from which we would proceed to our final destination: an air base in Italy.

When we arrived in Italy, we were to deposit our plane at an air base near Fogia, north of Bari on the eastern side of the Italian peninsula, and travel by truck to the 450th Bomb Group's base.

To my relief, the first legs of our journey, from Kansas to Maine, Maine to Newfoundland, went smoothly. As a neophyte, being responsible for what seemed like a huge and ponderous heavy bomber was an awesome challenge. Knowing that I was the product of a condensed training effort, I was assailed by frequent moments of self-doubt. I found it amusing when I recalled that in my home growing up every mechanical device was called a "machine," signifying that it defied understanding.

We had now come to the portion of our flight plan for travel from Newfoundland to the Azores, strategically located in the middle of the Atlantic Ocean. The base we would land at served as the refueling station for thousands of heavy bombers and other aircraft in transit to the European Theater of Operations. These islands belonged to Portugal, and using them to facilitate the Allied war effort had been the subject of intense negotiations about a year before, a process in which Winston Churchill played a major role. By using Lages Field in the Azores, it was possible to reduce the flying time between the United States and North Africa from seventy hours to forty.

That my nine crewmates were depending upon my navigational skills to steer us safely to a smidgen of land somewhere in the seemingly infinite space of the Atlantic Ocean was burdensome for me to contemplate. The metaphor "like finding a needle in a haystack" seemed an apt description for this circumstance. This was clearly not an assignment for a beginner. Another consideration, I gloomily realized, was the possibility that the weather conditions we encountered might prevent my use of celestial navigation—a sextant is of no use if stars are not visible.

It further undermined my peace of mind to be warned by the Gander navigational briefing officer that we could expect German submarines to sabotage our efforts to arrive safely. Lying in wait near the flight path, the submarines would frequently lurk beneath the surface in order to send false radio directional beams to guide planes away from the air base. They hoped to lead us sufficiently astray that we would run out of fuel and be forced to ditch in the cold water. Recently, several new bomber crews had already fallen victim to this ruse.

We took off from Gander in the early evening, anticipating that we would touch ground in the Azores at daybreak. Disappointingly, our trip had to be aborted after a half hour over the ocean—an inauspicious beginning. We were compelled to return to base for refueling because of a gaffe attributed to Mario Caserta, our flight engineer. A fuel storage procedure involving the transfer of fuel from the spare tanks to the main storage tanks in the wings had been mishandled, a mistake that required an additional day's layover in Gander before we could take off again.

The incident created a moment of awkwardness. Pissed off, Jim McLain berated Mario in no uncertain terms, revealing to the crew that our pilot was no pussycat, especially when it came to proper maintenance of the airplane as well as other matters related to safety. In time, however, Mario more than proved his trustworthiness as an engineering hawk eye, and all was forgiven in regard to this first misadventure.

Over the course of our many combat missions, we learned that we could all screw up on occasion, including McLain. The important thing, if we wanted to stay alive, was to recognize and analyze the source of our errors. Over time, we learned to be completely candid about what went wrong and introduced procedures to prevent repetition of performance mishaps. This attempt to maintain precision in our operations, we knew, might well save our lives.

On our second departure, I crawled into the nose compartment, swinging my body up through the front wheel entrance. My first task was to prepare my work station by laying out my maps, plotting tools, computational aids, and other paraphernalia of the navigator's craft. I knew I would be busy as hell all the way over. At takeoff, I sat with Mike on the pilot's deck and waited for the word to be given, once airborne, that it was okay for me to descend to my station. The plane rose smoothly into the clouds as we started our flight eastward.

Having earlier reviewed the navigational flight plan with Jim and Woody, I felt we were squared away for our journey. After a half hour's flight over the ocean, I observed that the stars were out, giving me a chance to establish our location. I peered out of the Plexiglas astrodome in the dark of night and with my sextant measured the altitudes of three stars. I plotted their lines and constructed a small triangle on my chart. If I was reasonably accurate in my sightings, we should be within the triangle.

Hurtling into space evoked within me a sense of awe and also a feeling of loneliness. The sky seemed to lack boundaries, and I felt as though we constituted a mere speck in the universe. I felt disconnected from anything that had come before this journey, including my past experiences within my family and all of the people I had been close to. At the same time, there emerged in the inner recesses of my psyche a romantic feeling of kinship with the navigators of ancient times who sailed the seas on frail boats exploring uncharted areas of the planet.

As the journey continued, I reported to Jim at half-hour intervals, giving him my plotted locations and estimates of the time of our arrival at the Azores. Communicating in this way over the intercom system allowed the crew to keep informed about our status. I followed this up by going to the rear of the plane for short breaks and chatting with the guys. Everyone seemed quite relaxed and upbeat.

Mario worked closely with the pilots, checking the functioning of our four engines and inspecting other operational features of the B-24, such as instrument readings, to make certain there was no oil leakage. He kept careful track of our fuel consumption. Hardly twenty years old, he showed great energy and boundless enthusiasm as he scurried back and forth on the plane. His assignment was critical to our safety, as he served as the eyes and ears of the pilot.

Mario was obviously fascinated with airplanes and seemed well suited for his assignment. During our crew training period at Biggs Field, he could frequently be seen studying the manuals carefully, and he talked often about the B-24 with our pilots, maintenance staff at the repair shops, and other flight engineers.

Born and raised in Bridgeport, Connecticut, Mario had relatives in Italy and hoped for a chance to meet them. He achieved distinction among us for the fact that he was carrying on a torrid romance by correspondence with a girl back home. The one comical ingredient to the relationship: He had never met the young woman. She began the correspondence when Mario's name appeared on a list of servicemen who desired to receive mail from a female at home. Pictures were exchanged, and the two appeared to like what they learned about each other. We teased Mario mercilessly about this goofy relationship, but he took it in stride. And we had to concede that in this topsy-turvy time of war, some of us had to get emotional sustenance from even the most unlikely sources.

Although they were close in age, the relationship between Mario and Jim McLain was more like that of father and son than brothers. Although Jim was hardly a martinet and capable of easy bantering with Mario, the taciturn seriousness commonly attributed to his

Scotch-Irish ancestors came through forcefully when the matter of proper maintenance of our airplane arose. We accepted that he wanted us to survive under his leadership and were not surprised when he rode Mario's ass from time to time with the most cutting comments if he discerned that a critical matter involving our safety was being handled casually. While we had affection for Mario and trusted his devotion to carrying out his assigned duty in conscientious fashion, it added to our sense of security when Jim dressed him down for failure to follow procedures as prescribed in the maintenance manual. We knew that seemingly trivial errors in judgment could result in disaster, and we accepted the validity of Jim's strict performance orientation. Our lives were at stake.

After several hours of flying in total darkness, I realized that the clouds had thickened considerably and it was no longer possible for me to navigate by celestial means. Further, it appeared these conditions would last for the rest of our journey. Since I was required to provide our pilots with headings that would allow them to compensate for the drifting effect of prevailing winds, I would now have to rely upon the wind estimates given to me in briefings hours ago at Gander Lake. This approach troubled me, because meteorological predictions were notoriously unreliable.

I made no mention of my concerns about the vagaries of our navigational situation; I didn't think it wise to create a sense of alarm among the crew. I treated the situation as if everything that was going on relative to navigational issues was normal. Secretly, I feared we were involved in a game of craps with the odds working against us.

Another hour passed, and it began to get light. With morning approaching, it was as if a veil had been lifted. Everything seemed fresh and beautiful, less gloomy than when we were floating in darkness. But the passage of time also seemed to have accelerated as I realized that we had come to that juncture in our flight when, according to my calculations, we should soon be seeing the Azores emerging below us. After considerable straining to spot our destination, I was crestfallen to find that there were no islands in view.

Jim's voice had an edge when he asked me whether we should maintain the last heading I had given him. Trying not to convey my sense of humiliation, I heard myself recommending that we remain on the prescribed course. My calm voice belied the inner turmoil I was actually experiencing.

Yet I had no alternative but to continue to rely upon the calculations derived from the wind directions and velocities provided in the meteorological forecasts given by the Gander weather people. I was stymied by circumstances beyond my control that could, I knew, consign us to a catastrophic end.

For lack of anything else to do, I began tracking white caps of waves on the ocean surface, using my drift meter for this purpose. I came up with adjustments in determining our drift and offered minor modifications in my instructions to Jim about the heading to take. But what I said sounded like bullshit to me, offering little certainty that I knew what in the world I was doing. I might just as well have held up a wet finger outside the window of the aircraft as the source of my information about the winds.

We were now almost one hour beyond our estimated time of arrival. The prospect that we would run out of fuel became increasingly real, and we began rehearsing ditching preparations. Pilot and copilot searched for the signs of radio signals from the Azores' air tower, to no avail. With our fuel dangerously depleted, a moment of truth took over and the crew became noticeably subdued. Communication over the intercom was at a minimum, as if everybody was holding his breath. The silence, freighted with morbidity, was sporadically broken by terse inquiries.

The intercom clicked on. "This is McLain. Dave, are you sure we are headed straight for the Azores? Your ETA is way off." A biting edge of sarcasm could be heard in his voice. We were faced with a monumental disaster. We were likely to end up in the drink!

The copilot spoke up next. "Woody here. Mario, what's your last reading on fuel consumption? How much flying time do we have left?"

Despite the fact that our predicament occurred through no fault of my own, I was left with feelings of profound personal failure. I figured my crewmates would peg me as a fuck-up, and the disgrace was hard to bear. I cursed the meteorologist who had briefed me at Gander, because his predictions were rubbish.

Although conscious of the hazard of receiving false signals from German submarines, we were desperate and tried to pick up radio communication from the Azores. After about ten minutes with no success, McLain reported that the radio had picked up English-speaking voices and that American-style music could be faintly heard. We had no alternative but to risk using radio beams to guide our flight path. The only encouraging note was that the signals seemed to be pointing us in the same direction I had specified. We proceeded.

Eureka! Jim said he thought he saw a land mass in the shadows ahead. After an eternity, the depressing pall that had hung over us was lifted. Indeed, the islands emerged in front of us as we passed over the cirrus cloud cover beneath our wings. With radio contact established, Jim informed the tower that we were dangerously low on fuel and requested that we be cleared for an emergency straight-in approach. Permission to land was given. When our wheels hit the runway a short time later and we rolled to a stop (which required Herculean braking action), we were freed from our crisis. We had just avoided an ignominious dunking in the Atlantic.

I suppressed my urge to pour out to my crewmates a litany of excuses for having subjected them to such a frightful ordeal. I wanted the facts to speak for themselves: No stars visible for celestial navigation; radio contact precluded by the presence of German submarines ready to give us false signals; no markers on the ground to provide clues of where we were; and poor meteorological forecasts on which to base decisions about what headings to provide Jim.

But everyone was exhausted, especially me. Instead, I chose to keep my mouth shut and resolved to redeem my reputation in the flying experiences that lay ahead. I was determined show that I was not a fuck-up.

The next day we flew to Marrakech, a port on the coast of Morocco. Taking sun lines with my sextant, I predicted our arrival at our destination right on the button.

Reputation redeemed? Maybe.

Note

The following is an excerpt from a letter I received from Jim McLain, written years after the events described here, responding to my request that he review the material in which I describe our trip to the Azores.

March 8, 1999
Probably because the Atlantic crossing was such a unique event, I have a vivid recollection of the entire flight from takeoff to landing. The fact that we were crossing the Atlantic Ocean at the same time, and within the same space as an extensive weather system, made our crossing a bit out of the ordinary. On course to the Azores, at sunrise, there was a substantial cloud cover above and below the altitude at which I had been cleared by military traffic control to fly.

When Dave informed me that we were well past our expected time of arrival at the Azores I could sense from the tone of his voice that he was concerned but not in a state of panic. As a matter of fact, I was not thrilled with the possibility of ditching in the ocean either. After recovering from the initial surprise, I put Dunwoody and Caserta on special watch from the cockpit to see if they could spot any sign of the islands.

I then turned on my cockpit radio and scanned the frequencies to see if I could intercept any radio transmission traffic. After several minutes, I picked up the sound of music on the commercial band. I listened awhile as the sound of American [U.S.-style] pop music was received loud and clear from a transmitter that was sending a very strong signal, possibly close to our position over the Atlantic Ocean. I simultaneously switched the radio compass and breathed a silent prayer that the transmission was from a friendly source and close enough to emit a reliable signal to follow to an island airport base and a safe landing.

The directional needle from the radio compass reacted positively to the strong signal and pointed about 75 or 80 degrees to the right of our course. I was looking intently in that direction when I saw what appeared to be land barely visible through a break in the clouds. I turned the plane to the radio compass heading and descended through and then below the clouds. After flying on the new heading for several minutes, the beautiful island and the airport appeared ahead of us.

The whole episode was the result of a combination of circumstances that were not supposed to have happened. We were delayed by mechanical problems. The need to get our aircraft and crew overseas to replace heavy combat losses in the 15th Air Force was so urgent that we were ordered to cross the Atlantic in submarginal weather. This was one of several occasions when we fully understood the meaning of the word "expendable." Dave managed to establish enough navigational fixes to keep us on a good course, but he did not have the continuing navigation position fixes to establish an accurate ETA. He did a good job with the limited information he had. Anyway, we did not know exactly how to get to our destination in the Azores.

Maybe it was simply a coincidence that I turned the radio compass to a commercial frequency of the G.I. radio station at the air base at the precise time to see land through a break in the clouds. That could be. Or our religious friends might suggest that God wanted to teach some hot-shot flyboys a lesson about arrogance and humility. Some irreverent souls might say that God was just having a little fun at our expense on a slow day. He sure got the attention of this Protestant, who believes that the preponderance of the evidence is on the side of our religious friends.

Jim's letter gives clues about the personal characteristics I admired about him when he served as first pilot of *Myakin'*. The pithy directness in the way he addresses issues and his understated humor are classic McLain. And clearly a highly intelligent mind organizes his observations—qualities that served our crew well as we flew through flak-filled skies over formidable targets in places like Ploesti, Munich, and Vienna.

Myakin' *in Flight (Photo courtesy 450th bombardment group website at www.450thbg.com.)*

11

A Chilly Reception for Replacement Crews

I Knew You Once

I knew you once upon a time,
Like I knew many more,
I think I knew your last name
Before I learned the score,
You worked and slept alongside me,
A member of the crew,
Not knowing you would soon be gone,
Your life would soon be through.
You did your duty on the gun,
You were good at what you did.
No one would think by watching you,
That you were just a kid.
I really don't know what it was
That hit you on that day,
No time to stop, we carried on

No one knew what to say.
Your place was filled by another kid,
Who looked about the same,
And now I wish I knew you then . . .
I wish I knew your name.

—Scott Aylesworth,
720th Squadron, 450th Bomb Group

It was a few days later that we delivered the B-24 Liberator bomber plane to an air depot near Bari, an Italian city situated on the Adriatic and the location of the headquarters of the 15th Air Force. Having carried our crew across the Atlantic, the plane would be fitted for combat flying and assigned to a group unknown to us.

After a day's layover, we set out by military truck to the 450th Bomb Group (Heavy) where we would be stationed, about five miles from Manduria, a town located on the main road between Taranto and Lecce. The group occupied an air base that was formerly a military air station constructed some years before by Mussolini's Italian air force. The airfield out of which this group operated bore the code name of "Frantic."

Our journey of about 125 miles took us through the Puglia region in the heel of Italy, where we gained our first impressions of the country that was to become our military home. We passed through an area of flat plains, mostly covered with patches of scrubby vegetation, and then past fertile-looking farms and olive groves. As we sped along, we caught glimpses of ancient-looking churches whose worn exteriors blended easily with the surrounding landscape. Often, the farmers working under the blazing sun laid down their tools to examine us with interest. Enthused by the display of our American flag and the military insignia on our truck, they gave us the V-for-victory hand sign made famous by Winston Churchill.

Fatigued from the demanding travel since leaving the States, I gradually lost interest in these sights and managed to doze for the rest of the trip. I was awakened as we arrived at the entrance to the air base, which was guarded by American military police.

To my surprise, the setting was bedraggled in appearance, and I had a sense that we were entering a gigantic junkyard. In his memoir, Vincent F. Fagan, the pilot of another replacement crew arriving at the same time, described the physical arrangements quite accurately:

> It was a miserable setup. Dusty, scraggly, carved out of a huge olive grove and surrounded by a decrepit rock wall; the runway was oiled dirt with large chuck holes, and the few buildings had been unpainted for years—straight out of Tobacco Road. There were no hangers for servicing airplanes—all maintenance was done in the open air—summer and winter. There were some old Italian barracks appearing to be in imminent danger of collapse. The twenty-eight hundred Americans who lived here lived for the most part in GI tents; a few entrepreneurs built stone houses. The balance who couldn't get a tent or a house inhabited the barracks.
>
> There was an open-air movie theater, an Officer's Club, and several mess halls and administration buildings inherited from the Italians.
>
> If this was what a victorious army looked like in action—what a shattering thought to reflect on what a losing German army must look like.[1]

I was assigned a cot in an old barracks set aside for flying officers, along with Jim McLain, Jim Dunwoody, and Mike Heryla. Mike's cot was next to mine near the front door, and Jim and Woody's about a half-dozen cots away. Some thirty-five men shared these quarters, each possessing a cot and a makeshift arrangement of footlockers and boxes for storing belongings.

Our crew's six enlisted men shared a tent several hundred yards away from us. The separation of living quarters and eating facilities between officers and enlisted men felt disruptive, splitting us up as a crew. We made it a point to hold on to each other, figuratively at least, through frequent informal contacts.

Arriving in the midst of the Mediterranean summer season, we would have to get used to hot, humid weather. We were instructed to take Atabrine tablets, a medication designed to suppress malaria, a disease still rampant then in southern Italy. The men who had been there for awhile had a yellowish glow to their skin, revealing the concentration of Atabrine in their blood. We were also encouraged to swallow salt tablets and quench our thirst often from water provided by canvas cistern bags suspended outside our quarters. The water tasted brackish because of the chemicals added for purification.

In becoming part of the 450th Bomb Group, we entered a self-contained environment with a distinctly masculine tone. With existence coarsened by life-threatening encounters on bombing missions, the strain was revealed on the grim faces that we encountered as we wandered around the base. Crude street language was heavily used by the men of all ranks, and every third word was *shit* or *fuck*.

It must have been during this time that the crew under Jim McLain was first assigned to the B-24 Liberator in which the majority of our combat missions would be flown. The identifying name *Myakin'* was the sobriquet derived from "my aching ass," the familiar expletive of American servicemen when under duress. Painted on the nose section was an accompanying figure of a donkey kicking its hind legs high into the air. The display was an example of "nose art," a popular art form in the U.S. Army Air Corps. Looking at the other planes spread around our base, one was more likely to observe scantily clad pin-up girls adorning the B-24's. Men about to fly on missions were in the habit of patting favored anatomical parts for good luck. While our plane was not decorated with a sexy human form, we nonetheless developed a fierce loyalty to our misbegotten beast of burden, which, over time, came to signify our cohesion and identity as a crew.

We newcomers were referred to as "replacements," a term that carried emotional baggage, defining us as filling in for crews lost in combat before our arrival. A bomb group such as the 450th had a complement of about sixty B-24's on hand. Each plane normally carried ten men aboard. Sometimes other personnel were added, such as a combat camera photographer, a crewman using radar equipment (called "Mickey") to get a fix on targets protected by clouds or smoke pots, or a visiting command officer at the colonel level or higher.

On most missions, twenty-eight bombers, assembled in four squadrons of seven planes each, went out as a group. "Maximum effort" missions were sometimes organized with as many as sixty bombers participating in the combat assignment. Such large-sized initiatives were mobilized against targets of special strategic significance, such as the oil-production facilities in Ploesti, Rumania; aircraft manufacturing plants around Munich; and railroad marshaling yards and oil-storage facilities in and around Vienna. When good flying weather allowed almost daily missions, the cumulative loss of planes shot down was more pronounced.

No longer a single crew in transit, we were looking forward to comradeship as new members joining the 450th. What we encountered, however, was quite the contrary. A foreboding seemed to pervade the base, generating a psychological atmosphere as heavy as the noxious effluvium of a swamp. Like us, the "old-timers" were mostly in their early to mid-twenties. Among them, they had a range of completed missions under their belts, and some were close to finishing their tours. Whether in the barracks, mess hall, or outdoor movie theatre, they looked at us glumly and did not go out of their way to include us in their conversations or make welcoming remarks. Avoiding direct eye contact, they seemed determined not to take notice of us. When we were engaged in some piece of unavoidable conversation, the intent of their communication seemed to be to convey the message that our chances of survival were "not worth shit." Such peevish treatment left a disquieting feeling in its wake, suggesting that unimaginable horrors lay in store.

My fellow newcomer Vincent Fagan observed that the chilly reception seemed to come straight from the commanding officer:

> It was customary for the C.O. to greet newly arrived pilots at any base with a few words of welcome, usually something to the effect that "we're happy to have you with us and you'll like it here."

Not so with Fearless Red [McGuirk], West Point '39. He stood up on the stage in front of the twenty-four pilots and copilots, flanked by the group intelligence officer and group flight surgeon, stared at us intently for a moment, and then he spoke. "Gentlemen, you are fresh meat," said McGuirk. "I'm sorry to put it that way, but that is the way it is.

"This bomb squadron is exhausted—we have flown thirteen missions in the last fifteen days; 723rd squadron is down to five crews when they should have twenty." [2]

Based upon his observations flying missions as a combat photographer with the 450th, Al Saldarini confirmed for us what we had experienced: new crews tended to be left to themselves for a long time after arrival at the base, pretty much isolated from other crews. In the face of such a frosty reception from the old-timers, the members of our crew drew closer together.

We were barely able to stow our things before we were thrown into the reality of flying missions. The 450th Bomb Group had a policy of giving individual members of newly arriving replacement crews the opportunity to fly a couple of orienting missions with an experienced crew well schooled in the responsibilities of combat airmen. This was especially valuable for the pilots, who were required to maneuver their planes into tight formations at assembly points over Manduria. But the policy was not always observed, because circumstances might not allow for such orientation flights. This was the case when recent losses of planes were heavy and replacement crews had to be pressed into service almost before they could get themselves settled in their assigned quarters.

A few days after our arrival at the base, I received word from Squadron Operations that I would fly my first mission with another crew the following day. Despite the long preparation for this day, the reality that I would be flying missions within twenty-four hours left me feeling a bit numb. I realized that I was experiencing anticipatory anxiety, and it took discipline not to reveal my state of mind to my crewmates.

Shortly afterward, a tall, good-looking fellow with a handlebar moustache entered our barracks and introduced himself to me as Ivan Crockett. He was the navigator on the crew to which I had been assigned. He told me that this would be his forty-eighth mission, two short of the quota of fifty missions that would allow him to go home. I wondered whether he felt nervous about being so close to the end of his combat tour. It would be ironic if he were to be shot down just when he was getting close to the finish line of the big race. Despite these thoughts, I was encouraged by the fact that here was someone who had a good prospect of surviving his tour of duty.

Crockett informed me that we would be leading our squadron of seven planes within the group formation, and that I would fly in the nose gun turret enclosure where, in addition to being on the lookout for enemy planes, I would help him spot the target. Because this seasoned airman was both self-assured and low-key in manner, I found myself feeling relatively secure in his presence.

It was still dark at 4:30 A.M., when the sergeant from Squadron Operations roused me along with all the others scheduled to fly that day. After washing up, but while still sleepy, I managed to drag myself to the mess hall where men assigned the day's mission ate in silence. The gloomy atmosphere made me wary about what I was likely to experience this first time out on a combat mission.

After a tasteless breakfast of cereal, toast, and bad coffee, I headed for the briefing for all the navigators. As I entered the briefing room, I noticed a large map attached to the front wall with a red ribbon tacked on it to display the assigned route of the day's flight. The group navigator, standing with pointer in hand, told us that our bombing target would be an airdrome in the vicinity of a city represented by a red blotch on the map, and described navigational checkpoints that could be used to zero in on the target. Large black letters identified the name of the place as Wein. From the mordant comments aired by the other navigators, it was clear that they knew this site quite well. Since I had never heard of a city with such a name, I assumed that the target was not a major one and gave myself hope that it was likely to be what the flyboys called a "milk run." Although still feeling somewhat guarded, I decided this was a fortunate way to get introduced to flying combat.

The group navigator described the target area and presented photographs of the facilities we were to destroy. A friendly escort of P-38 fighter planes would accompany us as we approached the target. Should the contingency arise, they would protect us from attacks by the German Luftwaffe planes. We were also alerted to areas in proximity to our flight path where our intelligence had identified concentrations of anti-aircraft guns organized by the Germans. If we had to leave the formation because our plane was in difficulty, our responsibility as navigators would be to guide the pilots so as to avoid flying over these areas. In the event that we had to bail out of our planes because of enemy-inflicted damage or other mechanical failure, we were provided with the locations of groups of Marshal Tito's partisans in Yugoslavia fighting the Nazi army on the ground. If it became necessary to ditch our plane in the Adriatic Sea, we would utilize our radios to seek the assistance of Air-Sea Rescue units positioned at strategic locations.

When close to the time to board the B-24 on which I would be flying, I gathered my flight bag stuffed with the paraphernalia I would require on the mission. Because it can get quite cold at altitudes of twenty thousand feet or more, I had packed a sweater, a flight jacket, gloves, and boots. For personal safety over the target, I took a flak jacket lined with steel layers and a scull cap similarly protected. A battle helmet made of steel provided additional head covering as a safeguard against flying fragments of German antiaircraft shells.

I had been trained to take care of my oxygen mask so that it did not freeze at high altitude with ice formed by nasal discharge from my sinuses. I also took K-rations and drinking water, escape maps printed on silk, and local currency. I wore a forty-five-caliber revolver in a shoulder holster at my side, although the possibility of using the weapon after parachuting was remote, since armed enemy soldiers or their local allies would kill me as a lone airman on the spot if I reached for my weapon. The last task of preparation was to check out a parachute pack from the squadron supply room.

A weapons carrier drove our crew to the tarmac where the maintenance staff was performing last-minute checks of the engines.

While we waited for the flare signal activating the flight to go forward, Ivan reviewed the planned flight path with me. Pointing to his map, he identified the initial point (IP) where the bomb run would begin and the route to the targeted aiming point where we would drop the bomb. The process seemed simple enough.

As the men grabbed last-minute smokes, I noticed that the bantering that went on seemed to suggest little nervousness about our pending venture.

When the flight authorization was signaled, I entered the plane through the nose wheel. Sitting on the flight deck until we reached our assigned altitude, I listened on the intercom to the interaction between the pilot and copilot as they confirmed that each designated item essential to the plane's functioning was in proper working order. This included a wide variety of mechanical devices and their specialized indicators, for example: master switches, battery switches and inverters, pressure in the booster pumps, carburetor coolers, and so on. The copilot replied an affirmative "roger" to the items on the checklist.

After about a twenty-minute interval, we finally rolled down the runway in staged takeoff's with the other planes in our group. Climbing steeply into the clouds stimulated novel body sensations, and I suddenly experienced myself as an insignificant particle floating among swirling airplanes. As our pilot circled over Manduria, I sensed that it required all of his flying skill to maneuver our plane into its assigned place in the crowded expanse of the skies.

It had been a long time since the early days in training when I experienced horrific bouts of airsickness. However, the turbulence we now experienced in the process of group formation aroused fear that I would disgrace myself on my first mission by upchucking my breakfast. The situation became acute when the prop wash of planes in front of us caused our plane to get caught in a downdraft and drop precipitously. Fortunately, the worst did not happen, and I comforted myself with the knowledge that, despite my queasiness, I had at least reached the point where I was in command of my stomach.

Seeing our planes lined up in their assigned positions and joined with two other groups in our 47th Wing created an impressive vision: eighty-four heavy bombers moving as one entity, reflecting the bright sunlight, creating the image of a huge bird in the sky.

When we reached our designated altitude of about twenty-four thousand feet, the pilot informed Ivan and me that it was okay to enter the nose of the plane below the flight deck. We headed for our stations, and I climbed into the nose turret where I would man the two 50-caliber machine guns and assist Ivan, working at the navigator's station, in identifying the target.

Using my maps for reference, I followed the formation's course over the Adriatic. After a short while, I found myself looking down at the mountains of Yugoslavia. While they looked quite beautiful and peaceful, I had to remind myself that there were German troops down below as well as their Croatian fascist allies, the notorious Ustachi. I had been warned that these guys would just as soon slit an American flyer's throat as look at him.

It was a long flight to this place called Wein, giving me the chance to get used to the sight of so many B-24's flying around our plane in a tightly organized formation. With an azure sky serving as backdrop, the planes' shining aluminum bodies struck me as beautiful—awesome instruments of war and ethereal objects at the same time.

As our formation lumbered toward the target, the droning sound of the engines lulled me into a dreamlike state. It was as if my brain sought an escape from the present reality. To energize myself, I focused on the possibility of encountering enemy fighters and I swung my gun turret back and forth. When I saw specks in the sky above us, I momentarily perceived them as planes of the Luftwaffe. I notified the pilot and was relieved when he cheerfully announced that they were the P-38 fighter planes there to protect us around the target. I found the presence of the fighter escort a reassuring thought.

Time continued to move slowly until the moment I realized that several hours had passed since we'd left our base in Manduria. We had only about ten minutes to go before reaching the initial point beginning our run to the chosen target. Action would soon be upon us.

From my catbird's seat, I could see groups of planes ahead of us bombing the target. In the wake of detonating bombs, black smoke rose amidst splashes of fire. The surrounding sky was alive with flower-like bursts of flak. The scene reminded me of the fireworks displays I used to see as a child on the Fourth of July during Fanshel summer sojourns in Coney Island. The major difference, I realized, was that I was now looking at the explosion of German eighty-eight-meter antiaircraft shells. I tried to repress my uncontrolled shivering as I realized we would have to fly through these threatening concentrations within a matter of minutes.

As chance would have it, there was a problem developing, and events were not running according to the briefing plan. The pilot announced that another group had intruded into our flight path, and our group had been crowded off the assigned bomb path. This left our group leader with a quandary about how to execute our assignment. Dropping our bombs on the designated airdrome was no longer possible, because there was no way for us to get back into the vast armada of aircraft participating in this effort.

There was a great deal of talk going back and forth among our planes, the pilot informed us; everyone was pissed off by the disorganization that had taken place. But the situation had to be resolved quickly and alternative targets chosen. In the end, half of our group bombed military buildings in an area adjacent to the assigned target while the rest of our planes hit administrative facilities in the center of the town of Markersdorf. With this first mission turning out to be a chaotic affair, I was left feeling somewhat bewildered about the techniques that were supposed to give discipline and coherence to this massing of airpower.

As our group pulled away from the main formation, altering our flight path, we could not avoid going over Wein. I was taken aback by the huge size of the city. Suddenly the realization sank in: This was a high-priority target area, and we were certainly not on the milk run I had anticipated.

In a moment, we ran into antiaircraft shells bursting around our planes. The explosive sounds of shell fragments hitting our B-24 made me lose all sense of composure. I could feel myself stiffening up. No question about it, the guys shooting at us from gun emplacements down below would like to destroy our plane. In the face of this threat, everyone's attention was highly focused and talk over the intercom was sparse. I knew that this had to be the most anxious time on a mission, but at the same time there was a calmness on board our plane that was eerie but also impressive. I was fascinated to observe that all the planes in our group were flying straight and level, and I marveled that the pilots did not swerve their aircraft to avoid the oncoming black bursts.

We bombed the alternative target with good results, and the pilot gave us the message we had been waiting to hear: "Let's get the hell home!" We returned to base in group formation without incident.

For the descent over Manduria and preparation for landing, Ivan Crockett and I seated ourselves again on the flight deck behind the pilot and copilot.

I welcomed the opportunity to chat with Ivan. I commented about my surprise that this place called Wein was so huge. It was obviously a densely populated area. And so heavily defended by flak guns! He stared at me with an expression of disbelief on his face. After a long pause, he burst into a paroxysm of laughter.

Ivan fairly shouted: "Wein? You really don't know what city you flew over? I can't believe it! Dave, you can write home that your first mission with the 450th Bomb Group took you over a place called 'Wein.' The name you saw on the map is the German name for Vienna, one of the most important cities in human history, capital of the Austro-Hungarian Empire, and now as rough a target as there is in Europe!"

Ivan then got on the intercom and let the crew know about my confusion. Everyone had a comment to make, and the guffaws were heard loud and clear. After we landed, the razzing continued as we lined up for coffee from the Red Cross van. I was reduced to a state of embarrassment, as I clearly perceived that my career as a combat airman had not gotten off to an auspicious start.

First, I have trouble guiding a plane safely over the Atlantic. And then, I cannot even identify one of the highest-priority targets. *Some navigator!*

A Chilly Reception for Replacement Crews

Having flown my first mission with Ivan Crockett provided me with access to at least one airman on the base who had had considerable combat experience and seemed open to conversation. Trying to make amends for having ridiculed me before his crew, he invited me to have a drink with him at the Officer's Club in the evening.

After the dinner meal at the mess hall, I strolled to the club, not much more than a long hut, where the men apparently gathered for socializing, particularly after missions. I also discovered that it was a place where a flyboy could meet nonflying officers, such as flight surgeons, intelligence officers, chaplains, and administrative officers. Occasionally, we were joined by the top brass from squadron or group headquarters, including those in the ranks of major, lieutenant colonel, and colonel.

Ivan and I began with an exchange of small talk about what section of the country we came from and what air bases we had been stationed at since entering military service. It turned out that both of us had trained in aerial gunnery at Buckingham Field in Fort Meyers, Florida.

Loosened up by one drink, it did not take me long to raise the question that had been on my mind since I'd first set foot on the base: "Why is everyone walking around here as if he has a hot towel around his head soaked with self-pity? Why all this doom and gloom stuff?"

Ivan smiled at the mixture of earnestness and naivete reflected in the way I posed my questions. He paused and seemed to be searching within himself for a response to my obvious ignorance. He told me in a gentle voice, "I can imagine that all this seems crazy to you, and I know that it takes some getting used to. This has to do with the fact that you don't have the pictures in your head that I do from the missions I've flown where I have seen all kinds of people, old-timers and fresh replacements crews, like yours, obliterated before my eyes. Some got hit on their very first mission and some on their very last."

Ivan ordered another drink for both of us and then let me know the score. "You come during this first week in July and you discover that an occasional plane gets knocked down by 'Fritz the fuse cutter.' And you wonder what the hell the big deal is, since the odds are pretty good that you'll come through the mission okay. One plane out of twenty-eight might not seem like such a high risk. You're likely to get a few flak holes in your B-24, to be sure, but these can be patched up overnight by the ground crew."

Ivan took a few pieces of paper from his shirt pocket. "I like to hang out at Group Intelligence and read the reports about missions." He stared at the notes he apparently had been keeping and then read me the bare facts, as if he were a certified public accountant analyzing the data on death and mayhem in the 450th Bomb Group:

"On May 30th, we lost two of our B-24's to flak while on the bomb run over an aircraft factory located at Ebreichsdorf in Austria.

"On May 31st, two B-24's went down from flak hits over the Romano/Americano Oil Refinery at Ploesti, Rumania.

"On June 9th, two B-24's were destroyed by flak flying over the airdrome at Oberpfaffenhofen in Germany.

"On June 13th, two B-24's were taken down by flak while the group was bombing the Allach Motor Works in Munich.

"On June 16th, one B-24 was lost under fighter attack over Bratislava, Czechoslavakia, bombing the Apollo Oil Refinery.

"On June 24th, four B-24's were downed by fighters over the Romano-Americana Oil Refinery at Ploesti, Rumania.

"On June 26th, two B-24's were shot down by flak over the Heinkel aircraft factory at Schwechat, Austria.

"On July 6th, one B-24 was missing from a bombing mission on a steel railroad bridge at Pitesti, Rumania . . ."

Ivan continued his recital. He told me that in the six weeks before I experienced my first mission on the day's flight to Vienna, the group flew an average of only two missions every five days. It was necessary to abort many efforts because rainy weather would have prevented a clear view of the designated targets. Yet the 450th had lost eighteen planes during that period—almost two-thirds of the normal complement of twenty-eight planes.

After listening to these facts and figures, I began to understand what Ivan was driving at: On a *single* mission, you have a good chance of surviving, even when one or two planes get shot out of the sky. This incidence of loss is only 4 to 7 percent of the group's combat formation. But if you have to go out for *fifty* missions before they'll send you home, the odds are strong that your plane is eventually going to suffer a fatal hit.

Ivan sardonically summed up his view of the whole business. "The crazy feature about flying combat is that knowing there is a strong possibility that violent death is going to take your life away on one mission or the next coexists with the fact that you can feel almost normal between missions. You learn to live in the *now,* and you can sidestep thoughts of danger. You comfort yourself with the knowledge that you are going to be alive for the next twenty-four hours, and you become quite relaxed.

"It is only when you are summoned to a mission briefing session in the morning and later pull yourself aboard the plane that your heart enters your mouth and a chilling fear penetrates the inner recesses of your body. This business of being secure one moment and apprehensive for your survival the next means that your psyche is blowing hot and cold throughout your combat career."

Ivan was silent for a short spell and gave the impression that he had become detached and was lost in thought. When he resumed talking, he got to the heart of what had been disturbing me. "You see, Dave, it is not just a question of having your own life terminated," he snapped his fingers, "just like that! The fact of my own likely death constitutes the ultimate scary outcome of a mission. No doubt about it. But it is also very painful to get to know a guy who has been sleeping on a cot next to you, someone you find you have much in common with and you share a friendship with that is becoming meaningful." I noticed tears welling in his eyes. "And then he's suddenly gone, as if he never existed. You see the Squadron Headquarters guys come over and wrap up his belongings. They go through his personal things with care and make sure his wife doesn't get the photograph of the girl in Manduria he has been seeing.

"Dave, by giving guys like you the cold shoulder, we're protecting ourselves from a lot of pain if we see your plane go down over the target."

This introduction to the forbidding climate of the 450th Bomb Group served as a milestone in my military experience. A person living under normal circumstances conducts his affairs with the assumption that life will be ongoing and relatively predictable. The conditions I now encountered would no longer permit me to feel this way. It was as if I had crossed a divide and had entered a netherworld where death and dying had become the central theme of existence. In my mind, this marked me as different from family and friends at home and from the nonflying men on the base who offered support services. It is how I imagine a patient with a terminal illness feels.

Notes

1. Vincent F. Fagan, *Liberator Pilot: The Cottontails' Battle for Oil* (Carlsbad, CA: California Aero Press, 1992), p. 6.

2. Fagan, op cit.

> IN HONOR OF THOSE WHO SERVED WITH THE
> 450th BOMBARDMENT GROUP (H)
> ITALY, 1943–1945 WORLD WAR II
>
> SQUADRONS
> 720th–721st–722nd–723rd
> "THE COTTON TAILS"
>
> DISTINGUISHED UNIT CITATIONS
> REGENSBERG – FEB 25th 1944   PLOESTI – APRIL 5th 1944
> 1505 MEN OF THE 450th BOMB GROUP WERE
> KILLED OR MISSING IN ACTION

Lobau, Austria, Oil Storage Facility Bomb Strike Photo, August 22, 1944

12

In the Vortex of History

Manduria, Italy, July 18, 1944: The day's mission had been scrubbed because of foul weather. I was hanging out in the barracks, trying to catch up with personal chores. The other flying officers were playing cards, writing letters, or resting leisurely on their cots. I felt listless, however, and found it hard to concentrate.

I noticed Cosimo, the thirty-five-year-old Italian civilian orderly, staring aimlessly through a window. He irritated me. Perhaps I felt antagonistic towards him because it had been rumored that he had been *molto fascisti* until the Americans came. I intruded upon his thoughts with a sarcastic question:

"So, Cosimo, how come you put your whole future behind a bum like Mussolini?"

He shrugged his shoulders and looked me straight in the eye with an expression of contempt. He responded *sotto voce:* "So goes the stream, so goes Cosimo."

Yeah. So goes the stream.

I realized that my jumping upon the poor bastard with a dumb question was a sure sign that I was in a funk. It didn't take long to figure things out. My state of mind was obviously connected to two events that had taken place during the past week.

The first had been a few days before, when I had witnessed firsthand what Ivan Crockett had told me of. On only the third mission our crew had flown since coming to Manduria, the lead plane in our formation was shot down before our eyes, and the grim reality of what might lie ahead for us had sunk in.

The downed plane was piloted by Bill Snaith. Prior to this disaster, Snaith had been the chief of operations of the 450th Bomb Group. When we saw our crew listed for mission assignment on the squadron bulletin board, we knew that it was Snaith who had made the portentous choice. Any mission we flew might be the one that consigned us to history. But we harbored no ill will about being ordered to fly to a formidable target like Ploesti, because we had high regard for Snaith as a leader. We knew him as a man who put his own life on the line by taking his full share of tough missions.

And so it was on this day. Deep in Rumania, Ploesti was on the top of the list for strategic bombing because it was a major petroleum-producing complex, and the Germans desperately needed gasoline for their tanks and airplanes. Snaith's plane took the lead.

The mission notes of our pilot, Jim McLain, describe the moment of disaster:

> Our plane is slightly to the rear and under Snaith's plane when he takes the hit. I am maintaining our position in formation by concentrating on the tail section and underside of his plane. There are several close, heavy bursts of flak, and instantaneously a horrific ball of flame engulfs the lead plane. Our formation continues the run and we rally off the target. It is the first time we have seen a plane shot down in flames.

In my navigator's station in the nose of *Myakin'*, I was in close proximity to Snaith's plane. In the moment of catastrophic destruction, his B-24 was transformed before my eyes from a powerful four-engine flying machine to a splash of orange-red paint brushed upon the blue sky. It was like Houdini's sleight of hand: "Now you see it; now you don't."

Seeing it for myself caused a grim realization to take hold: Clearly, there is no time to exit the plane when fuel tanks are penetrated by flak. Bombs and gasoline explode instantaneously, and men and aircraft disintegrate together.

The second event was the arrival of a letter from my father. He wrote emotionally in a confusingly expressed way about events happening to the Fanshels in Russia. Terrible news had come his way from who knows where. In an emotionally labile state myself, I examined the letter so hurriedly that I failed to fully comprehend what was agitating my father. Writing in English did not come easily to Hyman, because he had been too busy earning a living for his family to take formal English lessons.

"*But anyway,*" I reasoned, "*if he wants to write about 'terrible things,' he's picked the wrong time to bring such matters to my attention because I am not in the mood. What can possibly be more disturbing than seeing our lead plane shot down and ten men obliterated? And the same thing might happen to the crew of* Myakin'.*"*

I dismissively tossed the letter into my footlocker, where it was likely to be lost among my scattered belongings.

Later in the day, I calmed down and reconsidered my aloof behavior. A second reading of Pop's letter afforded greater clarity, and I understood that what it had to tell me was indeed dreadful. I became a more sympathetic son.

The letter concerned my father's family still living in Russia. When the family had broken up in 1919, after the Bolshevik revolution, my father's sister, Geitel, thirteen years old and an orphan, had been left behind—despite her protests—in the care of her brother Levi and his wife. Meanwhile, my parents, their two children, and members of my mother's family, after wandering in Europe for a year, eventually made their way to the United States.

For years after my parents' arrival in the United States, my father's brother and sister, Levi and Geitel, still lived in the vicinity of Odessa. From the manner in which I heard my father speak about the families left behind, it seemed the prolonged separation from his siblings gnawed at him and caused a gaping hole in his psyche.

Over the years, Hyman took upon himself a punishing self-condemnation for having abandoned his sister while he and other family members found a haven in the United States. This burden of guilt was reinforced when the German invasion of the Soviet Union took place. The area of the Ukraine where Geitel, her husband, Moshe, and their two young children resided came under the brutal domination of local fascists—a mix of Ukrainians and Rumanians—exercising police population control under the supervision of the Germans.

My father's letter informed me that Geitel's life had more recently taken on a harrowing course under the scourge of the German occupation of the Ukraine. I wondered how he had learned about his sister's misfortunes, since it was rare for letters from Russia to come to our family during the war. (My guess is that immigrants as a class of people have intelligence networks that can almost match in effectiveness the organized military intelligence efforts of powerful governments. They are resourceful in finding out what is going on with their families in their former homelands.)

Hyman had learned that as the German troops descended upon Odessa, the government shipped Geitel's husband, Moshe, without his family to a safe haven in Tashkent in the Asian area of the Soviet Union. He was given special protection in order to retain the use of his engineering skills, which were an asset in the national war effort. While there, he fell in love with another woman, took up residence with her, and in a relatively short time word came back to Geitel that Moshe, the father of her children, had abandoned her.

My father wrote that the disintegration of the marriage was followed by an even greater calamity. Geitel's two young children were snatched by Rumanian fascists in a local roundup of Jewish youngsters and slaughtered with masses of other assembled Jews under particularly gruesome circumstances. Hyman had been informed that his sister's grief was profound. She was inconsolable and on the verge of mental illness. In common with most parents who have suffered such losses, Geitel was unsparing in defining her own culpability in the events that had destroyed her children. She felt that she had left them unprotected, not fulfilling her basic maternal responsibility by doing whatever was required to prevent her children from being picked up by the fascist predators.

When I came to understand it, my father's letter left me shaken. In his mixture of improvised Yiddish-English writing, he was able to convey an intense anguish. He specifically addressed my status as an active participant in the air war against Germany and defined my purpose in being in Italy. Not having the foggiest notion of my duties as a B-24 navigator on combat missions against strategic targets, he nevertheless urged me to do everything I could to wreak havoc on the enemy, wanting me to kill all the Germans I could. Personally! It was as if he imagined me somehow throwing our five-hundred-pound bombs from our plane.

Being the recipient of such a passionate letter and struggling to comprehend what my father was going through, I was handicapped by not being accustomed to corresponding with him. Writing letters to a parent in our family culture would make it seem as if we were communicating as equals. This was unexplored territory for me, because we had never been intimates in a true sense. My father's authoritarian propensity had always been a problem for his children, especially his three sons.

Back home before the war, the verbal interactions between us reflected an underlying tyrannical imbalance in the relationship. What I would say to my father was most often influenced by the feedback I was getting. Further, the subject matter of his letter was getting into charged territory. Hyman's complicated feelings about having abandoned his sister was a topic he had never really shared with me. I only knew that before the war my parents often quarreled about my father's spending more than our family could afford by sending packages of clothing to his relatives in the Soviet Union, who were constantly writing about the harshness of their personal circumstances. My mother thought he felt guilty about his sister who, she suspected, was working him over emotionally in an area in which he was inappropriately vulnerable. Mom felt that his Russian relatives did not realize that we ourselves were living in hard times, particularly after my father's heart attack.

As I walked around the air base in Manduria trying to lift my mood, I realized that my thinking about my father reflected my underlying wariness about him accumulated in the course of my growing up in the Fanshel household. When angry, he would become enraged and lose control in dramatic and scary ways.

In the middle of the Depression, and with the family's economic circumstances a constant source of worry, my father was often in a foul mood. When we children violated his instructions, he sometimes seemed on the verge of becoming physically assaultive. I was conscious of him as a man of strong physique, and the intensity of his gaze, when he was angry, intimidated me.

My unease with my father was reflected in an incident that took place when I was a five–year-old being taken to Temple Emanuel in Manhattan. It was then, and remains, the most prestigious synagogue in New York City, attracting a wealthy congregation. We were going to hear a guest cantor of world renown, and we were late. Hyman was rushing us along, and while I badly had to go to the bathroom, I was reluctant to face his wrath by delaying us. I finally had a most inappropriate accident for a five-year-old. When he saw the telltale signs that I had wet my pants, he was utterly disgusted and we had to return home. From his point of view, I had ruined what was supposed to have been a beautiful day together. Experiences with him of this kind considerably reduced my self-confidence.

In standing up to Hyman, as she often did, my mother seemed to be recklessly throwing fuel on the fire being stoked within him. A middle-sized heavyish woman, Mom would plant her feet on the ground, legs spread apart, and look him squarely in the eye. She would then hurl colorfully phrased denunciations at him, replete with the most sarcastic Yiddish words in her repertoire. This was the biting Kratchman style coming to the fore. She mocked him for the self-pity he indulged in because he had to get up at four o'clock every morning to deliver produce to a dozen stores in New York City.

"This is your job as the father of four children. Stop crying about it! Do you want me to drive your truck for you?" I later came to understand that, for all her bravado, my mother was also scared, deep down, but she took courage in hand and told Hyman off in no uncertain terms.

I found Hyman's letter disturbing to me in ways I did not fully understand. I sensed that a paradox was operating within me. Here I was in Italy participating in the death and destruction associated with the Allied bombings taking place over German-occupied Europe. Dozens of flying comrades in the 450th had been killed in the course of a few weeks after our arrival as a replacement crew. And having seen Colonel Snaith's plane receive a direct hit with the apparent loss of all on board, I asked myself: *"Why should the news of the death of two children I have never met create such an intense emotional reaction?"*

For days after receiving my father's letter, I had weird dreams about direct encounters with him. Like the Hebrew prophets of biblical times, he shouted his cry of despair in the language he normally used with me. In Yiddish, the words confronted me in a more penetrating fashion than if delivered in his broken English. *"Meer muz harginin de Deitcher. Zey zennen merderers fun kinder. Zol zey farbrendt verren in gehenen!"* ("We must kill the Germans. They are murderers of children. Let them burn in hell!")

I did not mention my father's letter to any members of my crew. I reasoned that we were all honorable and had our own individual motives for flying combat missions in Italy. I did not feel comfortable in seeking to define for my crewmates the nature of their motivations for risking their lives. For some men of the 450th Bomb Group, it seemed to be a macho thing: "It is manly to engage in combat and fight for one's country. Combat is not for sissies." "The guys at school signed up and so did I." For many others, enlisting in the military was an expression of patriotism: "My country was at risk, and as a good citizen I had to participate in its defense." Some men presented a more self-serving stance: "I was going to be drafted anyway, so I chose air combat because something about it was more preferable to fighting in the infantry. It seemed to offer a cleaner life."

Self-conscious and unsure of myself, I did not think I could successfully convey to my crewmates an understanding of the hodge-podge of circumstances, foreign to their experience, that were background to what had taken place in our family. These men were more securely rooted in the native soil of our country than I. In this context, I recognized that they were not in Italy to save the Jews of Europe. I did not see this as an expression of anti-Semitism, but rather as a reflection of the irrelevance of the subject in their lives.

For all my fitting in with my crewmates—we really did get along with one another quite well—I lacked the self-confidence to convey the history of the Fanshels in a comprehensible form. I sensed that the exotic nature of the events experienced by my family would have an aura for them of life taking place on another planet: A family wandering in Europe for a year after the Russian Revolution; an aunt left in Russia whose two children are murdered by the fascists; and Hyman as the conveyor of this information.

My complicated relationship with my father reverberated within me throughout my war experience. In my ruminations about my family, Hyman clearly got defined as the bad guy. And yet I felt there was more to our relationship than my earlier rejection of his letter would indicate, and something within me argued for his receiving a better hearing. I realized that I did not understand his thinking very well. I sensed that in his growing up in Russia he was exposed to the kind of pain we Fanshel children were spared in America.

I felt somewhat encouraged that our relationship would become closer now that that my encounter with my father's expressions of his feelings in his letter had created a spark of understanding within me about his burning intensity concerning the history of the Jews as an oppressed people. The story of his family might help to explain much of his disagreeable behavior that made it difficult for me to feel affection for him.

But my reticence to talk with my crewmates about what had been churning within me struck me as a personal failure, and it was not easy for me to examine my reactions objectively. It was rooted in a childhood conditioned by powerful forces that were beyond my grasp to fathom. They seemed to have conspired to make me a stranger in the larger American scene in which I was now immersed because of the war.

"*Yes, Cosimo,*" I thought, "*so goes the stream. But its current carries in its rush the debris of the historical eruptions we have lived through. The flow of time exposes ravished bodies of children and the charred remains of downed aircraft and their crews.*"

Flying Officers of B-24 Myakin': (left to right) *Mike Heryla, bombardier; Jim Dunwoody, co-pilot; Jim McLain, pilot; and Dave Fanshel, navigator.*

13

Clearing Myself with God

Please, O Lord! Save my life!
For Thou art gracious and righteous.
Our God is truly merciful,
He is the guardian of the simple-minded.
Even when I was low, He raised me up,
My life is once again at peace.
The Lord dealt kindly with me,
He delivered me from death.
He removed all tears from my eyes,
And saved my feet from stumbling.
Once again shall I walk before the Lord
In the land of the living.

From Psalm 116

Upon meeting my fellow crewmates in Texas some months before, my first impression was that my being the only non-Christian in the group was no big deal. More important and more immediate, I felt, was how we worked together as a team to be as effective as possible in combat. As we continued to train together, we rarely talked about religion, and I was pleased to note that crew members appeared to accept one another with relative ease and good will.

But here in Italy, as we settled into our combat routines, my religious identity gradually emerged as a more complex phenomenon—for me at least—than my original conception would have it. Over time, I could not ignore the fact that some of my buddies had come from parts of the country where they had little, if any, contact with Jews. Evidence of ignorance about the customs of people from my background arose occasionally, albeit without any sign of prejudice, and my concern about "fitting in" continued to linger at a subliminal level, not totally thrust aside.

Once again, I attributed my feelings of awkwardness to the insularity of the social context in which I grew up, realizing that life with the Fanshels was not organized to make me feel secure with non-Jews. I relied upon humor as a way of concealing my insecurities about my possible status as an outsider. This was particularly the case when cultural differences emerged in daily interactions between myself and others in my crew, whether an incident took place in the barracks or on flights on our B-24.

For example, several months after we arrived at our air base I received a parcel of food from my mother. I immediately tore open the wrappings, anticipating that I would be able to offer the other flyboys some of Mom's home-baked cookies, always popular with the Fanshels. Instead, I discovered that she had sent a jar of pickled herring and a rather long kosher salami, favored gastronomical items among Russian Jews. But alas, it turned out that by the time the parcel had been delivered to me in Italy, the salami had turned green and no longer resembled anything fit to eat. Further, the liquid in which the pickled herring was immersed had been transformed into a corrosive chemical compound, easily mistaken for hydrochloric acid.

When someone noticed me gingerly holding the moldy salami for inspection, I jokingly described the offending object, quite smelly after its long journey, as an artifact retrieved from a sunken sailing vessel. The pickled herring, I explained, was a new secret weapon to be used against the Germans. The exposure of Mom's good intentions gone awry became an occasion for expressive humor in the barracks, but I could also sense that it created bafflement among my buddies about the nature of the Jewish diet.

A sense of my family's exotic background also emerged when I was occasionally asked by my crewmates about the derivation of my family name. "That's an interesting name you have there, Dave. Is it French?" In response, I candidly identified our designated surname as a gift from the immigration officer at Ellis Island and provided an imitation of my father's report of his verbal encounter with the federal interviewer:

Immigration Officer: "What is your name?"

Hyman: "Chaim Veinschel."

Immigration Officer: "Hmpf. That's not an American name. Your name is Fanshel. Spelled F-A-N-S-H-E-L. I'll write it down for you. That is your name."

Aside from these minor examples of cultural difference, I continued to feel there was good will between myself and the others. I was therefore caught by surprise when a member of my crew interjected a critical tone toward me in an informal conversation. I learned that my lack of religious observance had been noticed and was disturbing to this guy. My antennas picked up the subtext: "You are endangering the crew."

If I strip away the polite overlay in our exchange, the more direct communication had the following content:

> Everyone on the crew has made his peace with God but you, Dave. Let's face it, we are all concerned about the prospect of getting shot down. None of us wants to tip the scales against us, and that is why all of us go to religious services on Sundays. We all pray to God. That is, everyone but you. As someone who has not done the right thing by going to Jewish services on Friday evenings, you are tempting fate. You ought to consider that by your behavior you may be placing the rest of us at risk. If you get shot down because you have not cleared yourself with God, we will go down with you.

I was taken aback in being asked to account for my religious practices. Normally, I considered the matter of my participation in religious rituals nobody's business but my own. But I realized that my crewmate was expressing his sincere belief, and I found it hard to dispute the logic of his feelings from his perspective. He really believed that he could get killed because of my failure to protect myself. From what he had told me, I sensed that several members of the crew shared the concern. I could not ignore the criticism directed at me, something that could possibly cause a rift between me and my crewmates, and I decided to attempt to remove it as a bone of contention.

Yet accommodating to the concerns of the crewmate who spoke to me, and conscious that he indicated that he spoke for others as well, posed something of a challenge. I had not been an observant religious person since I was fifteen years old; by this time, I was now pretty much a confirmed nonbeliever. However, I had kept my views to myself, and I had not been carrying the banner of atheism as part of my ideological baggage. I identified myself as a "secular Jew" to others, because the Jewish identity of my family did not turn me off. By some complicated calculus, I had always reasoned that if I loved my family, I had to love their Jewishness as well. And I believed I did.

Other than observing milestones such as the circumcision of male newborns and the bar mitzvah ceremony when they reached thirteen years of age, the Fanshel family did not put religious ideas at the center of our thinking. There had been little family talk about the subject. While my parents were intensely Jewish, their orientation focused upon the cultural and political aspects of Jewish life. There seemed to be a mixture in the family atmosphere of some adherence to norms about religious observance and a gentle spoofing of ultraorthodoxy whenever it manifested itself.

Inconsistent with the laissez-faire attitude adopted toward religion in my family was the fact that my father was actually well schooled in Judaism and very informed about things Jewish. His Jewish education was probably the foundation of his formal education as a young child in czarist Russia. While growing up, I had observed that Pop seemed to know more than anyone I knew about most subjects that related to the Jewish experience. For example, he knew all of the good cantors in Europe and the United States, went to hear them when they gave public performances in New York City, and was on personal terms with a number of prominent figures in the cantorial world. Cantors occasionally stayed at our house when performing on the High Holy Days at our local synagogue.

Standing next to my father when he was praying at our synagogue on Rosh Hashanah and Yom Kippur, I was awed by the fact that he seemed to know the contents of the prayer book by heart. And I was impressed that friends singled him out for discussions of controversial matters dealing with religious doctrine.

Given my father's rich background in this area, it surprised me that there had been almost no attempt by my parents to influence me to accept the validity of religious perspectives per se. Neither had I ever heard within the family the notion that there existed a special moral code that distinguished us from non-Jews. Of course, we had been instructed to be good, honest, hard working, and considerate of others—the virtues children of most faiths are taught by their parents. But there had been no predilection to identify such views as uniquely Jewish, and I had not been raised with the warning that God was looking down on me ready to pounce on me for my transgressions.

Allowing Hyman to take the lead in discussing religious doctrine, my mother seemed to share his overall pragmatic approach. I recalled her whimsically expressing her philosophical stance: "While I do not necessarily believe in God, just so—it does not mean that I have to slap Him in the face, either." I saw that she played her cards in a safe manner and was careful not to create waves. Her focus in daily life was almost entirely directed towards insuring our family's survival in the secular world.

After considering the issue raised by my crewmate, I decided to accommodate to his viewpoint by going to Friday evening Jewish services at the multireligious 450th Bomb Group chapel. With my eight years of Hebrew lessons and schooling in religious texts, I was able to comfortably participate in the services. It came as a pleasant surprise to feel warmed by the experience of joining other men with similar backgrounds, despite my atheistic beliefs.

It was obvious to me, however, that there were philosophical issues of personal integrity involved in my participation in religious services as a concession to the concerns of others when this was in violation of my own beliefs. In the years leading up to this time, I had yearned for union with the whole human stream. It surprised me to find issues about self-identity reverberating within me in this context despite my assumption that everything in this domain had been resolved. I found it ironic that as a participant in a gigantic war involving peoples around the globe, my conception of who I was, the matter of my Jewishness, and how it was expressed in my presentation of self was still an area to be worked on.

After attending a number of Jewish services on Friday evenings at the chapel, I had a vivid dream dealing with my equivocal relationship with Judaism. I conjured a scene in which a group of prominent rabbinical scholars were convened as a gathering of sages to discuss how my being Jewish had become a matter of interest to a crewmate, and how the sages understood my response to his expression of concern.

The Gathering of the Sages

The rabbinical meeting takes place on a morning in a simple, poorly illuminated hall. I recognize the setting as the meeting room of the first Hebrew School I attended at age six. The furniture is worn, and the overall atmosphere of the setting is impoverished. There are eight gray-bearded rabbis sitting around a rectangular table. They have gloomy faces and seem determined to deal with my case in a no-nonsense manner.

Rabbi Akivah (leader): *Rabbunim:* We are assembled to consider this poor soul, David, whose attachment to his Jewishness is so *mishugah*. His insides are full of tugging and pulling. He goes off in all directions and is pathetic to behold. It is amazing that he does not fall apart. . . . Look at this situation in Italy where he is flying on a bomber plane that drops bombs on Hitler's war factories. At least he is straight about what side he is on in this holy war! He is one Jew among nine Christian men. To a man, they are connected enough to their own backgrounds to practice the faith of their parents and go to religious services on Sunday. They realize that they have to make their peace with God. When you are fired at by big guns on the ground, you can easily get shot down or blown up. But David, that *schnook,* he holds back from going to Jewish services and *kvetches* about not believing in God. What redeeming qualities can this misguided soul have? What do you say, Rabbi Ben Yehudah?

Rabbi Ben Yehudah (stroking his beard and struggling to organize his words): Well . . . Well . . . He is a more challenging example than appears on the surface. Over the centuries, our great teachers have taught us that man is often a complex creature, full of contradictions, and sometimes seeming beyond improvement. They urge us to dig deep into human behavior for those things that are signs of strength that might eventually bring them closer to our holy teachings. At least David complied with the pressures of his Christian crewmates to go to Friday-night services.

Rabbi Ben Shmuel (interrupting with annoyance): Not so fast with the compliments! Not so fast! What should we make of this "diplomat"? David goes to prayer services not from any inner conviction that expresses a realization that he might get killed any day and is frightened for his survival. He sees people dying around him on these missions. You would think that faced with this ultimate catastrophe, he would seek wisdom and solace, recognize the frailty of human existence, and seek the help of the Creator. No. He engages in mumbling his prayers, embarrassed to admit his fears openly and simply trying to ease the fears of his crewmates. Not his *own* anxiety. What *chutzpah* in the face of God!

Rabbi Ben Yehudah: Ah, you condemn him for "mumbling" his prayers, for saying words without meaning them—using God's gift for his own purposes. But remember, many of our people "mumble" their prayers. Listen to them, as I do, at daily morning services and on sabbath. They recite their prayers from memory, and they speed through page after page of text. Such a speed that it's like a racing car in a sports stadium. How much meaning can be attributed to automated-from-memory recitals? So David has lots of company from our steady, mainstream flock.

Rabbi Akivah: *Rabbunim:* Let us remember that even if David simply spills out the words as a sham performance, emptying the results of eight years of Hebrew lessons that Hyman Fanshel arranged for him, some benefit in his development might yet take place. Whether it is being called upon to read *Kaddish* at a burial service for a departed one, or on a more joyous occasion at the bar mitzvah of a loved child, he may be touched by the emotional feelings underlying the words. At such times an inner understanding might be kindled even in such unlikely a specimen as David and he might come closer to us. It is better to see the low level of performance, the recital of words devoid of content, than no connection whatever to the lives of practitioners of Judaism. Some of the beauty of the words may enter the inner recesses of his mind, and who knows when a tree will commence to grow where before there was only a tiny manifestation of a seedling.

Rabbi Ben Shmuel: With all due respect, beloved Rabbi, we should be careful about David. He is a crafty one. He changes his colors to fit the occasion. Sometimes he presents himself as a full-blown atheist, like those who exhale fire from their nostrils as they talk, the kind who thumb their noses at all we revere. On other occasions, he participates and recites the prayers aloud with all sincerity as if devotion comes naturally to him . . . You cannot trust him.

Rabbi Akivah: Spoken with penetrating clarity as usual. But there is another dimension to this incident in David's life. It takes place in the middle of a horrific war in Europe that is resulting in the cruel slaughter of so many people and is particularly painful for us to consider as Jews. We have lost so many of our people to the Nazi beasts. David is using his resources of personality and intelligence to cement his relationships with his crew. If he asserts his right to be an atheist and refuses to attend Friday-night services as a crew member actually requests him to do, he is acting in greater harmony with his own beliefs. But he might well be creating a barrier between himself and the rest of the crew. There is the danger of his being experienced as an alien presence, as a possible source of evil influence. What David is doing by going to services might be considered his giving a higher priority to their purpose in being in Italy together, to rout the killers of our people. These men have to collaborate under difficult, life-threatening circumstances. Words recited in prayer can have appeal. But perhaps we should recognize the deeds ordinary men perform, sometimes exhibiting surprising valor when called upon, as a demonstration of their adherence to a higher calling.

Rabbi Akivah stands up and moves away from his chair. There is a fade-out as he indicates that the gathering of the sages is over.

A summary perspective emerged for me as a result of my perusal of issues of religiosity and Jewishness while peeling the onion of my World War II experience flying missions on a B-24. I stood exposed by my ambiguous and pragmatic approach to the subject. I was obviously very different from those with clear orthodox views and their polar opposites on the determinedly atheistic side. This had historical roots and imitated the adaptive approach taken in my family. Stated in perhaps its most crude form, the Fanshel *modus vivendi* could best be described as follows: "*Religion is not an area in which you want to stick your neck out. Ambiguity helps placate the gods, and those who claim to speak for the deity. It is not an area in which ideological purity gets you anywhere you want to be.*"

A B-24 Dropping Payload

14

The Chief Currency of Life

Nobody wanted to talk about being scared. Our pride and self-esteem were involved, indeed threatened, and beyond that we had no useful vocabulary to describe such a state. How do you talk about fear when fear is fast becoming the chief currency of life?
—Robert Kotlowitz, *Before Their Time*[1]

As we gathered at the 722nd Bomb Squadron bulletin board, the familiar rumor that the next day would be a "big one" was tossed about with feigned indifference by those of us whose names appeared for mission assignment. Having become more seasoned in combat had helped our *Myakin'* crew to board our B-24 and perform our assigned tasks like old hands. But considering our discouraging prospects for surviving a tour of fifty missions—recent losses had been heavy—it was not surprising that there remained an underlay of tension that we carried within us even when we were not flying.

After dinner, I hit the sack early because I wanted to be rested for whatever lay ahead. However, sleep was fitful, and I tossed and turned. The mattress on my army cot provided little comfort, being nothing more than an assemblage of blankets scrounged from the effects of airmen shot out of the sky on prior missions. Some of the guys on whose blankets I now slept had disappeared before our very eyes as their planes disintegrated into flames. While we managed to go on with our routines without talking about our lost comrades, memories of their violent deaths often prevented Morpheus from performing his magic.

That night, I dreamt a scenario that had *Myakin'* shuddering eerily: We had received a direct hit from a German eighty-eight-millimeter cannon. The nose of the plane was violently thrust upward, and we came perilously close to a stall. And then what was most feared happened: We plummeted into a nosedive, straight down toward the ground; my stomach felt as if it was being yanked out of my mouth. I thrashed around in the nose section of our plane as I frantically tried to escape. But when I realized the situation was hopeless, I gave up and succumbed to the forces of gravity, awaiting the cataclysmic destruction of my life.

I was mercifully removed from this horror show when I suddenly awoke. Lying for a moment bewildered, I realized then I had only been dreaming.

It was undeniable that the cramped physical setting of our four-engine bomber plane contributed to the anxiety that existed within us, especially those of us working in the tight space of the nose. We realized that if it became necessary to bail out, we might find ourselves stuck in the confined space, unable to escape in time. On long flights of eight or more hours, it was easy to have the illusion of being interred in a tomb.

Thomas Childers, author of *Wings of Morning* (Addison-Wesley, 1995), wrote about World War II bomber plane exploits and described the environment of the B-24 quite accurately:

> Dubbed the banana boat, the flying brick, the pregnant cow and the old agony wagon . . . the B-24 was not built for comfort. Even entering the aircraft was difficult. The bombardier, navigator, and nose-turret gunner were forced to squat down, almost on hands and knees, and sidle up to their stations through the nose wheel of the ship. Once inside,

the three men, fully dressed in their bulky gear, would be squeezed into a compartment the size of a broom closet turned on its side. . . . The nose gunner was the first to climb in, squirming up and inserting himself into the nose turret. The turret was so compact that he could not wear his parachute when he closed the metal hatch at his back. Following him in, the bombardier took up his position at the bombsight just behind and below the turret hatch. . . . The navigator, the last to wiggle up into position, entered the navigator's tortuous station. A tiny retractable stool, too small to sit on, was built into the right side of the fuselage and the navigator's table, on which he had to arrange his charts and make his calculations, was little more than a thin shelf on the bulkhead that separated the nose from the flight deck. . . . While the bombardier squatted beneath him, the entire compartment was so unbelievably cramped it seemed impossible that three men dressed in cumbersome flying clothes could operate in such close quarters. Seeing it for the first time, the navigator understood why each crewmember had been tested for claustrophobia.[2]

The following morning, tension aboard the *Myakin'* rose as fifty-five B-24's lined up for takeoff—it was indeed "a big one." We were embarking on a bombing raid with the mission of destroying the Lobau refining and oil storage complex. Our target was seven miles south-southeast of Vienna, and we had almost double the number of planes usually mounted for a mission. Hundreds of powerful Pratt & Whitney engines revving up at once created a painful din.

Upon takeoff, our aircraft shuddered as we climbed, and we realized that our pilot, Jim McLain, was having a tough time maneuvering the plane into our formation of B-24's within the limited air space available over Manduria. Planes were bobbing and weaving around us, and the chaotic scene reminded me of Times Square at New York City's heaviest rush hour.

Like clockwork, our planes took off on each combat mission at about the same time every day. In the back of our minds, we were aware that our assigned route was likely known by the enemy, generating an unspoken fear. We felt certain that fascist sympathizers within the vicinity of our base in Italy were in contact with German outposts on the Adriatic coast, and that the men operating the Wehrmacht's artillery batteries were alert to the fact of our takeoff and that we were heading their way. While we sought to outwit our foe by feinting in one direction and veering toward another, we seldom succeeded: It seemed they were always ready for us.

Our mission, as set forth by 15th Air Force Headquarters in Bari, called for us to carry six 500-pound bombs. We were instructed to drop these powerful explosives on the strategically important oil storage facilities, six miles down the Danube from Vienna. With Ploesti having been captured by the Russians in their march through Rumania, the German military had been hard pressed to obtain fuel for their war machine, which was heavily dependent upon airplanes and tanks. Our briefing officer sought to reinforce our resolve by emphasizing the fact that raids on targets such as Lobau would provide much-needed assistance to the embattled Russian troops who were winning grudging respect from Hitler's military cadres.

With Ploesti no longer in German hands, Vienna had now become the most feared target for us flyboys. As one of the premier and historically important cities of Europe, it contained major war-related assets, such as aviation construction facilities, ball-bearing plants, petroleum storage complexes, and railroad marshalling yards that served as major distribution centers for supplying the German army. To defend such resources, the enemy had distributed a formidable array of flak guns in and around the city.

Fear focused our attention when massive firepower was directed at our formation flying at twenty-four thousand feet. Once we entered the bomb run, we had no recourse but to fly through the bouquets of exploding flak. A report from a pilot in a group following us in the formation lineup that day accurately described the scene:

> The first bombs had found their mark, turning parts of the target into a roiling inferno of flame and smoke. Four miles above the conflagration, vignettes of mayhem and carnage were playing themselves out in the flak-pocked sky. A plane in the lead group was the first casualty, sliding

German Antiaircraft Flak Viewed from a Plane

out of formation with two engines on fire. Minutes later, another Liberator lost half a wing, flipped on its back, and went into a mortal spin. Another took a hit directly amidships, plunging earthward with such force that both wings sheared off. Like a broken piñata, another split in half at the bomb bay, spilling crewmen as it fell.[3]

This surreal drama unfolded in a matter of minutes. As we approached the target, a heightened sense of personal danger began to paralyze my body. In the midst of the bomb run, and under continuous attack, I resolved to continue functioning by concentrating upon tracking navigational markers defining our location along the prescribed route. I knew that *Myakin'* could be lost just as catastrophically from navigational errors as from flak. If it happened that our plane became disabled and we were separated from our group formation, it would be my responsibility to guide us back to our home base in Italy. Becoming disconnected from our group's formation would put us at acute risk of being attacked by German fighter planes.

I managed to improvise a series of strategies that might permit me to control my fears, most of which ultimately proved unsuccessful. My effort to gain equanimity might suggest that I was engaged in a rational process that had been carefully thought out. This of course belied the desperate and chaotic circumstances that surrounded my quest.

As artillery shells burst around our aircraft, I first attempted to turn my brain off, to disregard the dangerous nature of our situation. I simply proscribed thinking that I might die at any second. My strategy was to dismiss dire thoughts and wait for the ordeal to end. I tried to put myself in a controlled psychic state in which no thinking was taking place. I posed like a piece of marble sculpture, like something in a museum, incapable of movement. I attempted to remove myself emotionally from the horror show that confronted us in the sky. But in a few minutes I realized that this employment of hocus-pocus in controlling my thinking was easier said than done; the strategy did not work.

I then moved on to assume the stance of a choreographer, because I realized that physical repose would help me cope better. I was aware that my body reflected how scared I had become; my back had stiffened into a tight vise, and I felt a spasm of pain. My neck seemed transformed into a metal pipe, and my jaw was clenched. I tried to shed this muscular straightjacket by forcing myself to move around in the limited space of the nose of the plane. I also practiced deep breathing, in and out, trying to compel myself to go limber. I told myself: "Relax!" In a short while, I learned that this approach was also ineffective.

I then engaged a problem-solving approach by concentrating on actions that would save my life in an emergency, such as preparing for disaster and getting ready for split-second responses. Where was my parachute pack? When would I attach it to my harness rings? Where and how should I exit from the plane? I kept my senses alert for sudden events that might require us to bail out. But, as with other strategies, I soon found that preparation had its limitations.

It occurred to me that what I needed to do was not fight death but rather embrace it. I must get to the bottom-line issue: putting death and dying in perspective. War or peace, we all must die eventually. Death is the main player in the human comedy we enter into at birth, and flying missions provided the basis for dealing metaphorically with death. Alas, I soon realized that I was engaged in pointless psychological drivel and abandoned this way of meeting my survival needs.

I finally became practical and hit upon something I could successfully carry through. I allowed myself to get lost in the details of my navigational responsibilities. As I saw it, the trick was to distract myself by keeping busy. I tracked where we were relative to identifiable sites on the ground. I obtained estimates of my wind directions using my drift meter and calculated the time of arrival for the release of bombs over the target and the time required for us to fly back to Manduria. I also focused upon my log-keeping responsibilities.

This strategy of keeping busy turned out to be the most successful. A clear indication that I was using this approach was reflected in the nature of my log keeping. I recorded my comments in great detail and carefully resorted to block printing letters. As antiaircraft shells burst around us, I concentrated upon my penmanship. My writing resembled an architectural draftsman's. In child-like fashion, I concentrated upon rounding circular letters, crossing my *t*'s, and dotting my *i*'s. I had regressed psychologically to the second grade at Public School 46 in the Bronx with Miss McCarthy coaching me.

My preoccupation with meticulous writing impressed me as ludicrous, and almost made me laugh. But it seemed the only way I could retain some degree of composure. I also provided elaborate narrative descriptions of all notable incidents occurring during the mission. I described the flight path taken by our group, the nature of the flak bursts directed at us, and the condition of the target area after our bombing. Everything I saw was put down to the smallest minutia.

We somehow managed to return safely to our air base in Manduria. When we jumped to the ground from *Myakin'*, we noticed that shell fragments had torn holes in the fuselage. Our aircraft looked as if it traveled through a terrific hailstorm where pellets of ice hitting our airplane had created holes the size of grapefruits.

We took comfort in the fact that we had survived another mission with nobody in our crew killed or wounded. But the 47th Wing, of which we were a part, had suffered the loss of seven bombers. Witnessing some of the stricken planes in the process of disintegration was very unsettling, and the size of our losses that day had an emotional impact. After a brutal mission like that one, crewmembers gladly accepted the two-ounce shot of whiskey routinely offered to us upon return to home base.

As I prepared for the debriefing conference with the group intelligence officer, I anticipated that my excessively elaborate log notes would be scoffed at as the unseemly behavior of a "brown-noser," a guy trying to score points with superiors. However, to my surprise, I received laudatory comments. I gathered that much of the debriefing material turned in on logs prepared by our navigators was unreadable and provided a paucity of intelligence information. This was understandable, because writing in cramped quarters at subfreezing temperatures, in life-threatening situations, was hardly conducive to bringing forth model prose and penmanship. But I took little pride in my obsessive performance, because I knew from where it came. Driven by intense fear, I had been behaving like a kook.

After a few weeks, something even more unexpected occurred. A communication was received at the 450th Bomb Group Headquarters, sent by no less a personage than Major General Nathan F. Twining, Commanding General of the 15th Air Force. It read:

15th Air Force Headquarters
COMMENDATION
1st Lt. David Fanshel, 450th Bomb Group, 722nd Bomb Squadron, is commended for his neat navigation logs
on missions to Vienna and Munich

When I comprehended that I had been lauded for being a *"neatnick,"* I was unable to restrain a raucous laugh. Miss McCarthy would be proud. The commendation demonstrated that if you are sufficiently terrified, and behave weirdly enough, you will receive your just recognition for stellar performance from the U.S. Army Air Corps.

Given the intense fear generated by engaging in bombing missions, a common experience among those involved, I often wondered why the men, myself included, did not refuse to fly. Yet the withdrawal from combat duty rarely happened. Giving in to the need for self-preservation in this manner was not acceptable. For me, quitting would have represented a self-inflicted wound, defined as a profound life failure. In the military culture of the 450th Bomb Group, I would have been regarded with contempt by my fellow airmen, a man reviled. More important, my personal value system would have lost credibility. I would not have been able to hide the odious definition of others from my own self-scrutiny.

I remember reading that the British felt the same way. They labeled those who withdrew from combat with the Royal Air Force by the epithet "LMF" ("lacking moral fiber"). This is not the kind of disparaging designation one wants to carry through life.

In common with my fellow crewmembers who served on *Myakin'*, I resolved to complete each mission to which I was assigned. In my case, I understood that this was not an act of personal bravery, but rather the motivated action of the non-hero. It was based upon a fatalistic resignation in the face of a reality that had a lock grip on my behavior, one that I could not resist. When push came to shove, the sense of shame would have been more unbearable than the physical destruction of my body.

Notes

1. Robert Kotlowitz, *Before Their Time* (New York: Alfred A. Knopf, 1997), p. 83.

2. Thomas Childers, *Wings of Morning: The Story of the Last American Bomber Shot Down Over Germany in World War II* (Addison-Wesley, 1995).

3. J. Merritt, *Goodbye Liberty Bell: A Son's Search for His Father's War* (Dayton, Ohio: Wright State University Press, 1993), p. 32.

Budapest Bomb Strike Photo

15

Last Days of the Budapest Clunker

Such then, I said, are our principles of theology—some tales are to be told, and others are not to be told to our disciples from their youth upwards, if we mean them to honour the gods and their parents, and to value friendship with one another.

Yes; and I think that our principles are right, he said.

But if they are to be courageous, must they not learn other lessons besides these, and lessons of such a kind as will take away the fear of death? Can any man be courageous who has the fear of death in him?

Certainly not, he said.

And can he be fearless of death, or will he choose death in battle rather than defeat and slavery, who believes the world below to be real and terrible?

Impossible.

Then we must assume control over the narrators of this class of tales as well as over the others, and beg them not simply to revile, but rather to commend the world below, intimating to them that their descriptions are untrue, and will do harm to our future warriors.

—Dialogue between Socrates and Adeimantus, Plato's *The Republic*

It was July 27, 1944, just two days before my twenty-first birthday. Participating in combat flights three or four times a week, I was becoming fully immersed in the war experience, and the weight of it made me feel older than my years. Thoughts about death were always with me, and I was quite sure that I was not the only one who felt this way. We knew that the statistical probability of completing our tour of duty without getting blown to bits or having to parachute over enemy territory was very low.

Once we boarded our B-24 heavy bomber and embarked upon an assigned mission, our survival was strongly influenced by the skill and judgment of our pilot, Jim McLain. It was he who had to maneuver the plane into the assigned position in the group formation to fly with the others as part of a unified effort. The group size of a given mission depended upon the orders received from 15th Air Force Headquarters in nearby Bari, and ranged from twenty-eight aircraft on a typical mission to as many as sixty on a special "maximum effort" undertaking. When we flew over the initial point of the bomb run as we approached the target, Jim McLain was required to adhere to the mission plan specified at the preflight briefing session, regardless of antiaircraft fire threatening to down us from the sky.

But the pilot could not be indifferent to the possibility of sudden death that might await us. Socrates raises the question in his dialogue with Adeimantus: "Can any man be courageous who has the fear of death in him?" Unlike Adeimantus, our answer was unequivocally in the affirmative. Each completed mission was proof that fear can be overcome. We subjected ourselves to the enemy's defensive firepower every time we undertook to bomb his prized strategic assets. However, sometimes there was more involved than simply laying our lives on the line. The fear of death generates an ethical stance among combatants that is not formally articulated in the military code. It maintains that dying because of grossly flawed reasoning invoked by superiors or because outrageously poor military equipment has been provided is a state of affairs begging to be altered by those asked to make the ultimate sacrifice. Simply put, the exigencies of war do not justify the squandering of young lives in the service of a pointless death.

The day's mission called for us to bomb the Manfried Weiss Armament Works located in the city of Budapest. It was a facility that made small and middle-sized weapons for the enemy, instruments of war to be directed against our troops. We readily recognized the importance of our mission in the scheme of things, but our spirits were not exactly buoyant, because *Myakin'*, normally assigned to us on a regular basis, would not be available for this day's effort. Our shining aluminum bird had been taken out of action to allow some long-needed maintenance work to be completed by Dewey, our line-crewman primarily responsible for its care.

In its stead, we were assigned an alternative plane that had been used in many tough missions and was by now a patched-together aircraft. Scuttlebutt among the pilots and engineers was that this Liberator bomber had seen its better days and was ready for the scrap heap. The plane had been impossible to repair adequately since a crash landing a short time before, and it had a reputation of being dismayingly unpredictable in its performance. Being required to fly this piece of junk to a well-defended target would surely put a luckless crew behind the eight ball.

After our 450th Bomb Group took off and the planes began to organize into assigned flying slots in the formation, Jim and Woody, our copilot, discovered that the rumors about this airplane were right on the mark. The surface control tabs resisted being trimmed to hold the plane straight and level in flight. It flew in a skid and was difficult to hold in formation. As the pilots struggled with the controls, I could hear Woody muttering, "This is a bitch to fly!" He and Jim agreed that the greatly impaired condition of the aircraft was not only dangerous to our own crew's survival but to the other airmen flying planes adjacent to us. It was a miracle that we did not collide with one another.

With much sweat and strain, the mission was completed without mishap, but our pilots were clearly exhausted by the effort to keep us in the formation. On the ground, Jim expressed his relief that this "clunker" was not regularly assigned to our crew.

On August 13, our crew participated in a bombing mission seeking to destroy gun positions held by the Germans at the naval port of Toulon. Located on the shore of the Mediterranean and bristling with heavy guns, this former bastion of French naval strength was strategically located in the path of the anticipated Allied invasion of southern France.

Jim's notes on the Toulon mission indicate that our superiors in the military command structure did not always appreciate a pilot's concern for the safety of his crew when his judgment contravened those who were issuing orders:

> This mission was a textbook raid from the beginning. There was no enemy distraction to hamper the bomb run. However, there was an incident that happened upon returning to base that is crystal clear in my memory. I was summoned to the Operations Room to see some major from aircraft maintenance whose name I don't remember. He was hot because I had rejected the "Budapest Clunker" airplane and transferred to our *Myakin'* before going on the Toulon mission. My explanation that no crew should have to fly a plane in that condition on a combat mission was useless. I was then ordered to fly the plane for six successive missions "as a lesson in the discipline of following orders." Although I considered this unreasonable, the military provides few options to following orders.
>
> The only way I could think of beating the system was to leave the plane at some distant friendly field at the first opportunity, in a condition that would make it extremely difficult to repair and return to our base at Manduria. As fate would have it, on the following day, our next mission to northern Italy presented an ideal opportunity.

On August 14, the *Myakin'* crew flew the "Clunker" on a group mission to attack gun positions on the shores of the city of Savona, Italy. Allied troops were advancing northward on the Italian peninsula, and our bombing of enemy artillery positions provided valuable support. Jim and Woody decided on the way to the target

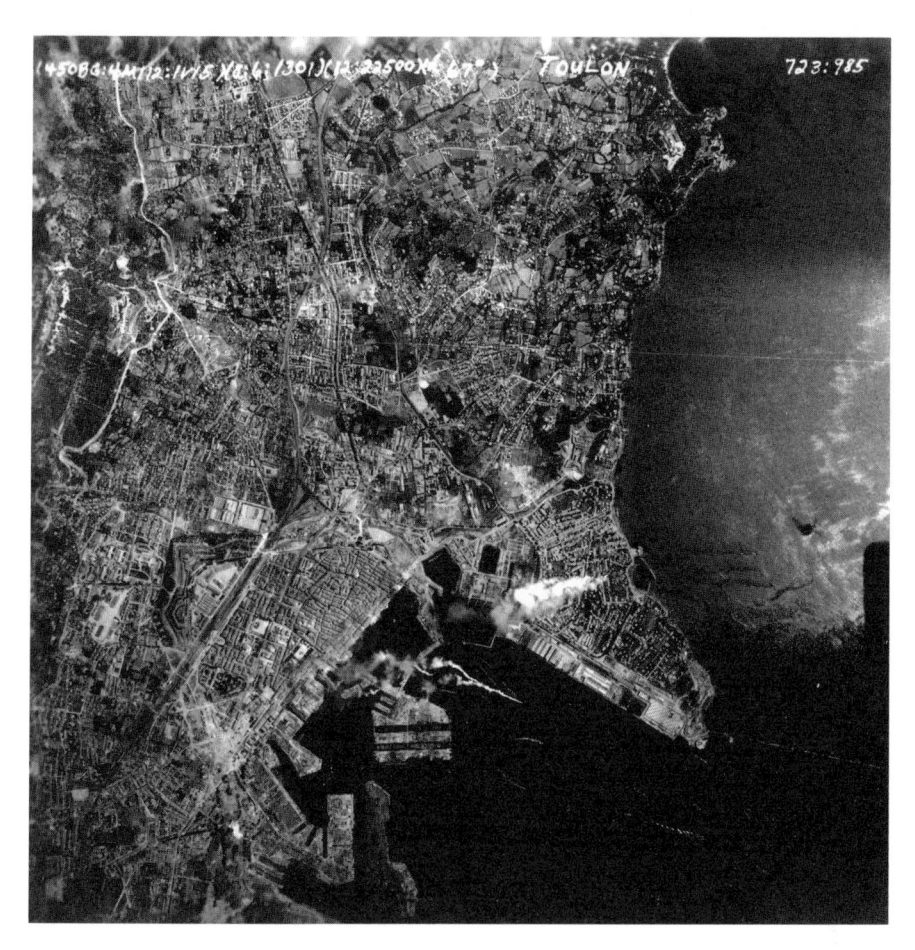

Toulon Submarine Pen Bomb Strike Photo. German Vessels are Fleeing from the Base.

that this was an advantageous time to get rid of the "Budapest Clunker" with which we had been saddled. Short and simple, they set the RPM and manifold pressure readings on the No 2 engine within a range calculated to cause an engine failure shortly after dropping our bombs. There was not too much concern of hampering us with an ailing engine, because it would be possible to retain our status within the formation on three engines. Jim McLain's notes tell the story:

Flak over the target is accurate and heavy. Three planes including ours are hit and damaged. The damage causes loss of power in an outboard engine but is not serious enough to require feathering the engine. We rally off the target with our box and a short time later leave the formation and head for the closest friendly field. Dave identifies the nearest friendly territory as the island of Corsica and gives me a compass reading. We begin a gradual descent to Corsica and reach the island with plenty of altitude left to locate a suitable landing site. Sighting an airfield, we contact the tower and tell the operator we have an emergency and to clear us for an emergency landing "straight in" approach. On final approach we are instructed to pull up and go around while a group of B-17's land. Woody comes back on radio with something like, "To hell with that, we have an engine failure, we can't go around. Repeat. Emergency. We are on a straight-in approach to the runway." We land with no problems as the B-17's pull up and circle the field. After we taxi to the Operation Building we inspect the aircraft. It looks like the fuselage has been dipped in engine oil. We are confident that the "Budapest Clunker" will not be returned to our base for a very long time, if ever.

    I sent a message to base that we had landed safely in Corsica. Operations told me that there was a B-24 on the other side of the island that I could fly back to Italy if I thought it was airworthy. We inspected the plane and we decided to fly it back to base. On takeoff, the cowling of Number 2 engine fell off but we decided to go on anyway. We arrived in Italy after dark. Everything was blacked out until we sighted a British airfield. Unable to contact them by radio, we buzzed the field to let them know we wanted to land. We were given a red light (No!) each time. On the third pass, we landed anyway, spent the night and traveled by truck to our base the next day.

    I gratefully remember that we never had to fly the "Budapest Clunker" again.

My recollection is that we flew in *Myakin'* on every crew mission after the Corsica episode.

The 722nd Squadron commander, Col. McWhorter, thought we were lucky to survive with no serious consequences and gave the crew some time off to recoup from the Corsica episode. So far as I know, neither he nor anyone other than our crew had any idea of how we deliberately trashed that aircraft.

Fast Forward to 1994 . . .

Over the five decades that have elapsed since the circumstances involving the "Budapest Clunker," the experience had remained hidden from my memory, lost among the myriad incidents that had greater claim upon my awareness. Normally, my attention gravitates towards phenomena that were more suffused with emotional content. For example, I have no difficulty remembering planes blowing up over a target or those that crashed on takeoff with parts of the aircraft landing upon our barracks. I also remember the times when red flares were released by flak-battered aircraft returning to our base with wounded men aboard. Even less vivid scenes are retained in memory, such as sights of solitary planes falling out of formation because flak had disabled them; forsaken by us, they were forced to fly home in grave danger of assault by enemy fighter planes. These images are not eradicated over time and are available for recall many years after the events took place.

The "Clunker" tale was first jostled in my memory in January 1992 when Jim sent me his diary notes about each of the missions our crew had flown. Reading his material, I felt a stirring of familiarity. I remembered that we had landed on the island of Corsica, and that I had identified the site as an appropriate place to land and provided the navigational headings for getting us there.

The incident joined one of about a hundred "nuggets" of memory, threads of loosely intertwined images that emerged from musings about events that happened long ago during my Italian sojourn. My interest is stimulated by the fact that some lessons of life are lurking below the surface of these fragments of memory. I wonder what these specifics of the war experience convey about me as a twenty-one-year-old actively participating as a combatant in a major war in Europe. Less narcissistically, I wonder what is revealed about the nature of military life that so powerfully impacted our psyches. There seems to be a lack of resolution in my thinking about important ethical and philosophical dilemmas encountered by young Americans like myself.

It was not until I focused upon the "Clunker" event that I came to realize that the story is compelling because it brings to the surface a critical issue that arises in the conduct of military operations. There was a struggle going on as to whether the combatant should totally lend himself—even at the risk of death—to the authority structure of a military organization in a war we have come to define post-Vietnam as a "just war" or a "good war." In competition to this orientation is the strong need to modify military orders in order to preserve one's own life as a participant.

From this vantage point, the Toulon mission turned out to have a special character in the history of our crew. It revealed Jim's leadership qualities in a way that exposes an approach to this central issue of military discipline that is laden with philosophical complexity. He exhibited courage in being fully committed to our effective participation in the overall military purposes of missions assigned us, balanced with a rejection of senseless risk to the human lives of the men under his command. The experience, years later, enables me to examine the principles guiding the behavior of combatants in warfare.

As a way of probing an admittedly complex issue from the more objective status that comes with my retirement years, I resort to the ploy of imagining here the incident of the "Budapest Clunker" being discussed in a student seminar of fourth-year cadets at the United States Air Force Academy in Colorado Springs. I envision the discussion being focused upon combat organization and the task of maintaining discipline in the command structure. The instructor is attempting to provoke thoughtful examination of the behaviors shown by an aircrew in a combat situation.

LAST DAYS OF THE BUDAPEST CLUNKER   *197*

The scene is set in a seminar room in the Air Force Academy, with five student cadets and an instructor seated around a conference table.

Captain Smith (instructor): For today's seminar discussion, I am assuming you have performed the assigned reading of a memoir written by a participant in an aircrew flying combat missions on a B-24 Liberator bomber in the European Theater of Operations in World War II. Although the incident we are examining took place decades ago, the issues remain pertinent for the current period. The task before us is to try to understand how those who are asked to carry out orders cope with the demands made upon them. What should we expect of young airmen—whose average age at the time was about the same as yours—who were called upon to deal with orders from superiors that impressed them as being unreasonable, and which they saw as a threat to their own survival?

To get us started in our discussions, I ask you to address a central question for our seminar: Is there any justification for "working around" orders given by a superior as was acted out in this case?

Cadet Jones: Sir, there is no issue here. It seems clear to me that these guys were in direct violation of the rules of military discipline. The decision to disable their B-24 amounts to the destruction of government property. The B-24 was a four-engine heavy bomber—an expensive piece of equipment. How can you conduct a successful war if pilots take it upon themselves to make such an aircraft inoperable for future use? This strikes me as a gross violation of the military code. If it happened under my command, I'd hit them hard with all the rules in the book. I'd make an example of them.

Captain Smith: John, you have a troubled look on your face.

Cadet Crane (struggling to organize his thoughts): Sir, I agree that what the *Myakin'* crew did was very unusual. The behavior does indeed have the distinct aura of insubordination about it. But I am troubled by the fact that the aircraft assigned to the crew apparently handled so badly in formation flying that it was a struggle to keep it straight and level. The pilots may have felt they were risking a possible collision with the other planes participating in the mission. This combat crew was faced with a very awkward situation, and there should be some concern about the poor support given them.

Captain Smith: Mary, you seem to be agreeing with John's statement.

Cadet Williams: Well, sir, I find myself worrying about the major in charge of maintenance. He seems to be overreacting when he orders this crew to fly six more missions in a plane they felt was totally unreliable and not safe to fly in combat. Somehow, this pilot appeals to me as a leader. He comes across as a thinking man not seeking to evade the dangers inherent in carrying bombs to well-defended targets. But he is also placing great value on the human lives involved. His attempt to be a problem-solving pilot is a praiseworthy attribute. Probably the German flyers in a comparable situation, flying in support of the Nazi cause, would not dream of resisting authority in any fashion.

Cadet Jones (unable to conceal his annoyance): I think we are losing sight of basics here. Are we condoning a system where every pilot can pick and choose his aircraft, seeking only the best equipment for himself and his crew? Let me say something on behalf of the major, who is being portrayed as the "bad guy." Maintaining these bombers under the miserable conditions that prevailed in territory recently freed from enemy hands was probably as vital for the successful conduct of the air war as was the care and feeding of the crews. He had an extremely tough assignment.

Captain Smith: Mr. Lopez. What do you think of all this, José?

Cadet Lopez (shy but smiling): I did a stint as an enlisted man before coming here and got to know the informal system pretty well. Sir, without being disrespectful, my guess is that this kind of behavior takes place within all kinds of military units, not just aircrews. It is likely that there are lots of orders given by superiors in warfare that tend to contradict the truths learned out in the field by those who have to carry out the actions. For example, newly commissioned officers arriving to take command in combat infantry units probably rely heavily upon seasoned noncommissioned officers who are experienced in battle. This makes sense and probably saves lives. The trick to operating this way successfully is to carry out the correction in a manner that does not cause the superior to lose status.

Cadet Jones: Sounds underhanded to me.

Cadet Lopez: It all comes down to "detectability." McLain and his crew did what they felt was necessary without their superiors being aware of what was going on. The approach worked. The *Myakin'* crew did not have to take unnecessary risks by flying in a plane that was dangerous. But it was important that their act of getting rid of the "Clunker" was not done publicly so as to stimulate wholesale maneuvering among the crews for planes that seemed to be in better condition. This crew, in fact, apparently did go on to complete a full tour of combat without further incident.

Captain Smith: Billy, you have been showing interest in the geopolitical aspects of World War II. What are your thoughts?

Cadet Martin: Sir, I've been trying to understand this episode in the context of what I have read about what was going on historically. I gather the Russians had long pressed their U.S. allies and the British to open what they called a "second front." In their eyes, the recent Normandy invasion was welcome but came late, and they were disgruntled because they, the Russians, had gigantic bloody battles going on and felt they had suffered a disproportionate share of casualties. In one of President Roosevelt's meetings with Stalin, he tried to placate "Uncle Joe" by promising to support the Russian offensive in the east by depriving the German war machine of military supplies. Relentless bombing of the enemy's military production resources—arms factories, petroleum plants, and so forth—would also support the Allied offensive on the ground in France.

I can imagine there was a chain of instructions from FDR to General Marshall, to "Hap" Arnold, commander of the Army Air Force, to General Twining, chief of the 15th Air Force, to the 47th Wing, down to the 450th Bomb Group. The commander of the 450th probably put pressure on his maintenance officer to mount maximum efforts. As aircraft maintenance officer, you scored points with superiors if you got sixty bombers up in the air instead of twenty-eight. This probably meant that standards of safety applied by the maintenance people were shaved down to a minimum. Planes like the "Clunker" were thus assigned to crews like McLain's despite their combat worthiness being severely compromised.

Cadet Crane: I've been thinking about what we would consider appropriate behavior if we were in the position of the *Myakin'* crew. If it was our understanding that being ordered to fly a defective plane for six missions in a row was actually consigning us to a high likelihood of death, how accepting would we be this outcome? We've been taught for four years now to be absolutely responsive to the leadership of our superiors. Yet the maintenance officer was not exactly a fount of wisdom. He probably was responding to the pressures from above to field a full complement of B-24's into the air ...

Captain Smith: Mary has something to say.

Cadet Williams: I find myself thinking about the possible reactions of my parents if they were to receive word that I had been killed in action and later learned I had been shot down in a defective plane. Would this be preferable to being informed that I was up for court martial for defying a superior's order? Even my father, an old play-it-by-the-rules army man, would probably prefer that I come out alive by resisting unreasonable orders than being totally compliant and paying with my life by being letter-perfect. Further, there is a strength here personified by the pilot that probably reflects a phenomenon that typifies the way Americans conduct themselves in many areas of life. We should appreciate the fact that these men were not totally cowed by authority. They were unorthodox in the way they went about it, true, but they somehow managed to get their input into the equation. I would say McLain had panache as a leader.

Cadet Jones (mockingly): "Panache?" Oh, boy. Fancy language—What does that mean?

Cadet Williams (stares intently at her interlocutor, then, after a pause, comments poker-faced): It means the man has balls.

(Seminar group breaks out in loud, unrestrained guffaws.)

Captain Smith (after sixty seconds of silence): Sounds like this head twister has become too taxing for some of us. We'll have to end the discussion here.

Class disbands.

This didactic seminar discussion treats the issue in a way that glosses over the emotional content of the events as faced by individual crew members such as myself. If asked: "Would you rather McLain had played by the book and not improvised an approach to bypass the major's edict?" my response is quite clear.

Belatedly, I can say: "Thank you, Jim and Woody, for taking personal risks that may have saved our lives. From my perspective, your behavior was cool."

Myakin' *Flying in Formation (Photo courtesy 450th bombardment group website at www.450thbg.com)*

16

The Fickle Finger of Fate

Crew members often referred to the "fickle finger of fate," a cliché applied to the air war when seemingly irrational things occurred in almost random fashion. Doubts about what unforeseen threatening developments we might encounter in weather, enemy resistance, or the functioning of our aircraft added to an aura of quirkiness about flying missions.

Instant Response: An Imperative of Survival

The hazard we feared most was that antiaircraft artillery guns shooting at *Myakin'* would cause a fire to break out. From the outset, we were highly aware that our plane's tanks stored a great quantity of combustible fuel that enabled us to fly to distant targets. Because when we were on a mission we flew unswervingly straight and level over the bomb run, we presented a stable target for German antiaircraft gunners on the ground to accurately track. A piece of flak penetrating a fuel tank would cause a catastrophic explosion—leaving no trace of our presence in the sky, only a puffy white cloud, something we saw time and time again.

An ominous incident occurred aboard the *Myakin'* during a major raid directed at the Messerschmitt aircraft engine factory in Munich, Germany. A piece of flak hit an oxygen storage tank in the rear of our plane, causing a sheet of flame to sweep through the bomb bay. Waist gunners Harold Lopeman and Whitey Martin were firsthand witnesses to the path of the blaze and alert to the possibility of imminent disaster. Flight engineer Mario Caserta was in the bomb bay area inspecting the plane and was also startled by the sight of flames.

Luck was with *Myakin'* that day, and the dangerous eruption of fire was gone within a minute when the oxygen was depleted.

While the short-lived crisis was going on in the rear of the plane, none of the crew members on the flight deck or in the nose section had any knowledge of how close to being blown up we had been. Only after we landed at our base in Manduria, and stood around enjoying coffee and doughnuts at the Red Cross truck, did I learn that a bizarre event had taken place on the mission.

"Whew! That was something scary," said Harold, shaking his head. "I don't know how we managed to survive."

"When that flame shot through our main section from front to rear, I thought we were doomed," agreed Mario.

"You bet! I clamped my parachute chest pack on my harness rings so fast I could have bailed out within seconds," added Whitey. "The fire seemed to envelop us."

Harold vented further. "I never thought I would see a piece of flak hit an oxygen tank and create such an astonishing blaze and still come out alive! It was something. Seemed like the flak could ignite our gas tanks, and, if it did, it would have been *finito* for us."

It surprised me to hear the vivid accounts of high drama to which we in the front of the aircraft were not privy. "We didn't have any idea this was going on with you guys," I said.

Harold explained how close he came to bailing out. "I looked out from the waist gun station and was ready to dive right out! The fire seemed to swirl around my ankles. But I looked down and held myself back before jumping. My thought: 'Hey! There are German soldiers down there. Maybe I should wait a few seconds to see what happens?' "

I inquired grumpily of Harold: "Why didn't you let us in the nose section know there was a fire in the back?"

"No time. No time . . . " His voice trailed off.

It was not until years later that I came to understand that the obligation of individual participants in air missions to alert fellow crew members about emergency situations is not an absolute requirement in the military code. In the face of fire aboard a plane, there are times when, in the interest of personal survival, there may be compelling reasons for the individual to urgently seek escape from the aircraft.

In a memoir about his experiences flying missions, Vincent Fagan, one of our pilots in the 450th, recounts that the subject of appropriate behavior in such crisis situations was addressed in an orientation talk by the group commander.

> Speaking to new pilots of replacement crews arriving in Manduria some time after we had begun our tour in July 1944, the commander said:
>
> "Here are a few things that may help you. Back in the States they taught you what to do in the way of emergency procedure in case an engine catches on fire. Personally, I've never seen anyone put out a fire on a B-24, and if one I'm flying in catches fire, I'm going to jump immediately. If you want to go through all the emergency procedures crap before you jump, it's all right with me. You have only four or five seconds to get out, though."
>
> A copilot leaned over and muttered, "A B-24 is just a bonfire waiting to happen."[1]

Miracles Sometimes Happen

The terrible reality of sudden death caused by antiaircraft artillery flak had been firmly impressed on our minds during our third mission on July 15, 1944, when our crew participated in a bombing raid on the Ploesti oil-refining complex in Rumania. I and members of our crew had witnessed Lt. Col. Bill Snaith, the chief of operations of the 450th Bomb Group, shot down with his crew in the lead plane of the mission. As new participants in the air war, it was an experience I remembered vividly.

So it is understandable that I was taken aback a month later to see Colonel Snaith walking around our air base! He had apparently survived the downing of his aircraft and was one of a group of prisoners of war returning to Italy from Rumania. They had been freed from their German captors by the advancing Soviet army and flown back to their bases in planes sent by the 15th Air Force. At the time I heard no explanation as to how this could be. Over the years, I never was able to fathom how a man could survive the instant disintegration of his airplane.

Eventually, I discovered a description of how Snaith came to be saved in a memoir written by William Cubbins, a pilot of the 450th Bomb Group. Cubbins had been shot down over the same target on July 3, 1944, two weeks before Colonel Snaith took the hit. He was housed in a prison established in a former Rumanian school building about a mile from the city's Opera House. He describes the dramatic circumstance under which he met Bill Snaith as a newly arrived prisoner:

> A shout announced the arrival of a new group of "criminals." They were a sorry-looking lot, sauntering along between two lines of armed escort. It was a large group, in triple columns, perhaps forty of them, led by a mummy. Despite the new bandages wrapping both hands and his face and head, there was something familiar about the mummy's frame and gait. I leaned through the loose barbed wire and sang out the familiar, "You'll be sorry!" The mummy looked up, peered at me through black eye holes, and answered.
>
> "No sorrier than you, Cubbins."
>
> His voice told me his identity. It was Bill Snaith. There had been several occasions during the two weeks since I'd been shot off his wing when I wondered if he'd made it. . . .
>
> Several days later, he related the details of his being shot down. He had led the strike on Ploesti on July fifteenth. Seconds after releasing his bombs, his aircraft

had received a direct flak hit in the bomb bay. The shell had turned the ship into an inferno. Unable to get out of the cockpit, which was filled with searing flames, he'd sat back in his seat, covered his face with his hands, and waited for the release of death. At almost that same instant, the ship exploded, killing his crew.

His first conscious thought had been the discovery that he was falling on his back, about two hundred feet below the flaming wreckage of his aircraft, and faced with a terrible dilemma. "If I pull my rip cord, will the wreckage fall on me? If I don't . . . ?"

He'd taken the only option available. He grasped the D-ring and pulled. His body was instantly decelerated by the deploying parachute, and the wreckage passed harmlessly overhead before falling through his altitude. But that had not been the end of his ordeal. Being the mission leader, and landing near the target, he'd had to endure the thundering destruction of the bombs of the groups that followed the rest of the Fifteen's hundreds of bombers on an all-out attack.

The Rumanian soldiers who captured him turned him over to the German defenders of Ploesti. That was fortunate. German doctors treated his burns before passing him back to the Rumanians.[2]

Snaith had survived in the face of almost total disaster because of the circumstance that pilots were the only members of the crew who did not wear chest packs as their basic parachutes, which required the crew member to clamp the packs onto their chests in emergencies. In contrast, the pilots wore backpacks in their seated positions, perhaps because it was expected by the designers of bomber planes that pilots would have to be the last crew members exiting their planes when enemy action had destroyed their capacity to stay afloat, and they would be the least likely to have the time to secure the pack to their parachute harness. In an unconscious state after the plane exploded, Snaith was evidently blown out of the plane with his parachute ready to be deployed. An extraordinary turn of events indeed.

A Rendezvous with History

The 450th took off on a mission on Sunday, September 24, 1944, as one of three bomber groups belonging to the 47th Wing. We were headed for the Kalamake Airdrome on the outskirts of Athens with a goal to destroy German planes on the ground as well as storage facilities for the enemy's military supplies concentrated near the airport.

While we had been cautioned in our mission debriefing to protect the famous archaeological sites of Athens, it nevertheless felt strange and burdensome to be flying over such a sacred city with full bomb loads. That I should find myself flying towards such an important historical site fascinated me. As a freshman at the City College of New York, I had participated in a course in philosophy in which Athens was extolled with lavish praise as the birthplace of important cultural and political developments in human history.

The political situation that surrounded our mission was unknown to us at the time, but years later the full purpose of our effort was revealed in history books on World War II. It would appear that the war situation in the summer of 1944 had created strains within the anti-German alliance. The Russian army had recently taken Bulgaria from German hands, and their armies were in hot pursuit, aggressively challenging the enemy's control of Greece. With the Axis foe forced to evacuate this important strategic asset in the Balkans, Churchill was anxious to guarantee that the status of Greece be secured as part of the British-American sphere of influence rather than coming under Russian control. This accounted for the fact that on this mission, we were engaged in an unusual two-tiered military operation. Each of our B-24's was carrying eight 500-pound bombs to be dropped on designated targets within areas of the airdrome. At the same time, each plane was assigned to pull a British glider in tow, an unusual activity for us. The gliders were transporting British soldiers, who would secure the area abandoned by the Germans.

Without engines to power them, the gliders needed to be lifted off the ground when we took off from our runway in

Manduria, and we would then pull them as tethered troop carriers to the target area around Athens. The plan was for the gliders to descend to the ground after being disconnected from our planes, and the troops would then disembark and take physical control of the airport. After releasing the gliders, our B-24's were to execute the plan of dropping the bombs on such German assets parked on the ground as planes, tanks, and other forms of military hardware.

During the days before the mission to Athens, the 450th was host to the British soldiers who would be transported to the gliders attached to our B-24's. There was an exchange of good fellowship with our visitors, and I found myself enjoying the camaraderie with them very much. I marveled at their high morale since they had been engaged in warfare for five years, a long time to be away from their homes and families.

The operation went as planned, and we released the gliders over the Athens airport; they were able to land without incident. Our group then flew over the specified targets, and Mike released our bombs in unison with the lead plane of our bomb group. Looking down at the target area, I saw that the bursts were accurately placed so that the storage facilities for supplies needed by the Germans were engulfed in flames. I made note in my navigator's log of our good results.

As we rallied off the target, our waist gunners sounded an alarm, informing us that one of our bombs had failed to fall freely and had been left hanging in the bomb bay, precariously wedged across the top of the catwalk. The fuse, primed before the bomb run for explosion on impact, could plausibly detonate if prop wash from planes in front of our formation severely jostled our plane.

As our bombardier, Mike was in charge of dealing with this crisis, and he proceeded to the bomb bay to attempt to defuse the bomb by reinserting the fuse pin. We watched his efforts with concern, and an eerie silence reigned on board *Myakin'*. Even if we safely sailed through the violent air currents, catastrophic impact would be a conceivable hazard when our plane struck the runway upon landing at our air base in Manduria.

A number of us stood by in order to be available to Mike if he required assistance as he worked. We marveled at his apparent calm as he stood in the exposed bomb bay with freezing winds swirling around him. He was wearing an oxygen mask attached to a portable tank, and as he examined the suspended bomb he resembled a creature from another planet. He studied the scene intensely for a long time before making his move. He had to prevent the armed fuse from spinning off on its own if the plane encountered treacherous air currents.

We sweated out the situation for awhile and were relieved when Mike reported that he had been able to reinsert the fuse pin and that he believed that the bomb would not explode even when the plane shook. However, he also told us that despite much effort, the bomb was too tightly wedged in the bomb bay to be dislodged over the Adriatic Sea as hoped. On return to our air base we would just have to land with the big guy and hope for the best.

When we finally arrived within the vicinity of our air base, Jim McLain consulted with the officers in the control tower and explained that we were flying with a five-hundred-pounder in our bomb bay, and while the fuse pin had been reinserted, something unpredictable might yet occur when we landed. Jim was instructed to keep *Myakin'* in a pattern away from the approach to the field until all the planes in the formation had landed and parked some distance from the runway. Other parked planes and vehicles would also be removed from proximity to where we would be landing. Ambulances and fire trucks would be on standby with personnel ready to act promptly if needed.

When cleared for our landing, Jim and Woody attempted to make this the smoothest landing possible. To their chagrin, however, our plane's touchdown with a gentle approach was still sufficiently jarring to produce an unpleasant result. The bomb came loose, went crashing onto the runway, and was bouncing head over heels behind us! None of us had to be told what had occurred, because we could see that the personnel, lined up with jeeps ready to help us, including British personnel, were running frantically away from the runway.

Good fortune smiled on us. With the bomb pin in place, there was no explosion even though the heavy explosive was subjected to a massive beating. The armaments crew was able to arrange for its transportation to an isolated site, where it was detonated without harm to personnel or valued structures.

This was an occasion where coffee and doughnuts from the Red Cross truck did not meet the need. The two-ounce provision of whiskey routinely handed out after each mission was supplemented with second swigs from a bottle saved for such an occasion. Toasts were lifted to *Myakin'* and our pilots—and to the "Brits" who had been fighting this war so long and made wonderful allies. Skill and luck had helped save the day.

Notes

1. Vincent F. Fagan, *Liberator Pilot: The Cottontails' Battle for Oil* (Carlsbad, CA: California Aero Press, 1991), page 6.

2. William R. Cubbins, *The War of the Cottontails: Memoirs of a WWII Bomber Pilot* (Chapel Hill, North Carolina: Algonquin Books of Chapel Hill, 1989), pp. 178-79.

Dave Fanshel at the End of His Tour of Combat Duty

17

Goodby, Manduria

Maybe sixty missions were too many for the men to fly, Colonel Cathcart reasoned, if Yossarian objected to flying them, but he then remembered that forcing his men to fly more missions than everyone else was the most tangible achievement he had going for him.
—Joseph Heller, Catch-22[1]

In mid-December, I finished my last mission by flying to an oil refinery on the outskirts of Vienna. It was the type of strategic asset that was always strongly defended by the Germans. As usual, the flak came up at us hot and heavy over the target, and shell fragments tore holes in our aircraft. Fritz the fuse cutter was displaying good aim that day. Luckily, none of our planes were shot down.

I was feeling hopeful. There was a sense of personal drama going on for me, because I was conscious of the fact that I had only a few more missions to fly. In a celebratory mood, I accepted the two-ounce shot of whiskey routinely offered all returning aircrew members after each mission. It was the first time I had accepted the offering, and I gulped the contents of the glass in one swallow. *Salut!*

The day proved to be significant in the history of my military service. Not yet revealed to me, fate had determined that my tour of combat duty would be over with this mission. The following day, I learned that a new accounting system for determining the completion of combat duty had been put in place as ordered by Nathan Twining, commanding general of the 15th Air Force. When our crew first began our tour with the 450th, fifty combat missions were required to be flown before an airman could be relieved from duty. The accounting scheme called for most missions to be accumulated as singles, and very extended flights to be credited as two missions. Thus, places like Ploesti, Vienna, and Munich were recorded in our personnel files as double missions. The rationale was that such targets not only required longer flights but likely involved the most dangerous encounters with the enemy. Indeed, we often came back to our air base in Manduria feeling exhausted by the demands of these double-headers. By this reckoning, I was credited with forty-seven missions, with eight sorties receiving double credit.

Within days, the new system was put in place, and we were told that henceforth all future sorties flown by us were to be credited as single missions and the standard requirement for ending combat duty would now be thirty-five sorties. By the new count, I had finished thirty-nine sorties. *Hallelujah!*

The end of a tour of combat duty held a special kind of mystique. Most of the airmen were superstitious about the possibility of being shot down on the very last mission. It had been known to happen. I construed the change in rules as amounting to my having been given a precious gift: I had flown my last mission without knowing beforehand that I did so.

Instituting the new system did not, however, signal the end of duty for others of the *Myakin'* crew. I was departing earlier than my crewmates, because I had been credited with additional missions flying as a navigator with other crews. These extra flights took place when I was assigned to the 450th Bomb Group's lead planes on special sorties. Sometimes, I was the lead navigator responsible to guide the group to the targets, and on other occasions I sat in the nose gun turret as a second navigator to assist in spotting the designated factory, distilling plant, or bridge to be bombed.

While the change was enthusiastically approved by all who had to fly missions, there was an occasional negative backlash from the top brass. This affected me personally when I found myself castigated by Lt. Colonel William McWhorter, the commander of the 722nd Bomb Squadron.

The incident took place on the first morning after I was taken off the flight roster and allowed to enjoy my new status. In his standard manner, the squadron orderly marched through the barracks at 4:30 A.M. and issued his clarion call for those scheduled to fly: "Mission is on!"

I relaxed in the pleasure of knowing that I would not have to fly on the day's mission. Even while I was aware of the rumor that returnees would be assigned to fly combat on B-29's over Japan after time off for rest leaves at home, I reasoned that whatever would happen a few months from now was not worth thinking about.

I was not totally submerged within my own concerns, however, as I observed fellow airmen, many of whom were friends, putting on their flying gear and stowing their parachute chest packs, K-rations, and escape kits in their flight bags. They were getting ready to place their paraphernalia on the trucks that would take them to the B-24's being warmed up for the mission. The men readied themselves to get some breakfast before proceeding to the mission briefing. I empathized with them, since I well knew the state of mind that took hold when preparing for combat flights. Deep down, a lack of ease pervaded the inner recesses of everybody's psyches.

On this occasion, our 722nd Squadron was scheduled to lead the group, and until the day before, when I was taken off combat duty, I had been assigned to fly as the navigator in the lead plane of the 450th Bomb Group with McWhorter. When he learned from the operations officer that I would not be flying on the mission, he became enraged. Being compelled to fly with a less experienced navigator evidently infuriated him, and he gave dramatic expression to his feelings by marching to our barracks. As McWhorter entered the door, the heels of his cowboy boots made explosive sounds on the floor, and the steady cadence of strident steps through the parallel arrays of army cots communicated his mood and authority.

McWhorter scanned the barracks, and when he spotted me, he hastened to my army cot to confront me as I lay reclining with a carefree expression spread upon my face. As they say in the ranks, I no doubt looked like "a cat eating shit." He did not conceal being pissed off at the sight of me stretched out like a sultan, and positioned himself in close proximity. His face settled into a fixed stare, and the attention of all in the barracks was focused upon him. It grew eerily quiet. After a few moments of silence, I erased the smile from my face and acquiescently rose to my feet.

In his cock-of-the-barnyard swagger, our commander finally allowed words to pour out of his livid face. Speaking hoarsely, he said, "Fanshel! Don't tell me that you're gonna take advantage of a fucking change in the rules and chicken out from finishing your full mission count. You're gonna save your sad ass just like that?"

The Southern accent of his verbal blast transformed him in my psyche, and he transmogrified in my mind into the head of a Cossack pogrom-making party in the Ukraine, as frequently described by my father in my growing-up years. He was poised to perform mayhem to another hapless Jew, ready to eviscerate my guts.

I struggled to keep my feelings under control. I gazed at him with a straight face and softly replied, "General Twining seems to think that my thirty-nine completed sorties are more than adequate, sir." I had invoked a higher authority and we both knew it. Checkmate. There was nothing my would-be-tormenter could do about my situation. Clearly exasperated, McWhorter stared at me for about thirty seconds, and, with the air lying heavy between us, he finally turned on his heels and stormed out, muttering choice profanities as he left.

In pondering my commander's outburst, and in the safety of his absence, I was inclined to use one of the picturesque curse phrases often used by our copilot, Jim Dunwoody, describing the fornication of two animals of unlikely match.

But I simmered down and attempted to put the issue into its proper focus. To engage in false heroics by flying three more missions to appease a man like McWhorter would be stupid. Like everyone else who has gone through the emotional grind of flying combat missions, the last six months had been the most challenging I had had to face in my young life. Each time we had gone out to bomb a designated target, it was with a sense of foreboding. Would this be the one in which our plane would be whacked out of the sky? The snuffing-out of our lives? McWhorter be damned!

My comfort in rejecting the idea of extending my tour of combat was supported by my knowledge that the odds of surviving fifty missions in the 450th had been quite dismal. Until recently, relatively few of our airmen had succeeded in reaching the requisite number. Of the men in the first sixty-two crews that had begun their tours in January 1944, about twelve (19 percent) had completed their missions and returned home safely. The other crewmen were either killed in action or wound up as prisoners of war in German-occupied Europe. In the span of time during which our *Myakin'* crew had flown missions, approximately the second half of 1944, the survival rate of individual flyers had been about 35 percent.

Post-War Musings

Although I am writing about this war experience in the context of my senior years, I vividly remember my encounter with my squadron commander. His verbal attack threw a momentary damper on my sense of celebration at the end of my tour of duty in Italy. His attempt to cast an aura of illegitimacy upon my ending of combat duty was uncalled for and abusive. But I had mixed feelings about McWhorter, since I shared the perspective of our crew that respect was due him. In our experience in flying under his command we found him to be a courageous leader, even if a bit of a grandstander. On one memorable occasion, he led our squadron over Munich's railroad marshaling yards when the other three squadrons of the 450th had aborted because of difficult weather conditions over the target. He had justification in avoiding flying through very heavy flak, but he held fast to the goal of effectively completing the assignment.

I discuss in various areas of this memoir the conflicts every military person experiences in going forth into dangerous situations. A well-established orientation in the military culture requires the individual participant in war to put himself on the line and behave bravely. This prompts the combatant to be motivated in his behavior by the higher purposes of the war as, for example, put forth so strongly by Franklin D. Roosevelt and Winston Churchill. The second common understanding of the human condition, however, sees the combatant as behaving with the basic impulse to save his own life. Most of us are not suicidal, and avoidance of circumstances that realistically raise the prospect of our dying is basic to the way we conduct ourselves. True, there are issues in war that require the individual to subordinate considerations of personal survival. But extending one's tour of duty as proposed by McWhorter seemed beyond the boundaries of what is required for honorable performance of one's assignment.

A residual issue for me, personal in nature, focuses upon Colonel McWhorter's negative reaction to me as an individual. Having to replace the navigator in his plane was a commonplace event and hardly justified a degrading public spectacle. Why was he so peevish over a trivial matter? I then, and now, sensed there was a Jew-hating impulse motivating his assault. We were vastly different in cultural backgrounds, I from a Jewish-immigrant district of the Bronx and he from the Southwest, probably Texas. I assume I was running into a core of bigotry in him that came naturally to someone of his background. I felt that he probably detested Jews. That was why I fantasized him in the role of a Cossack, a military guy bent on wiping out a person inherently distasteful to him.

Seeing myself as a victim of latent anti-Semitism came naturally to me, since the orientation conformed to the social scene in the United States when I was growing up. In the adult world, many occupations were not open to Jews, and there was exclusion from hotels, country clubs, and private beaches. In my own family, my brother had graduated college in 1937 as an engineer only to find that employment was widely denied Jewish engineers. At the local level, I had frequently run into physical conflict with Irish kids who lived near me in the Bronx and went to the Roman Catholic School across the street from my public school. The taunt of "Christ killer" was often hurled at the likes of us.

On my side of the interaction with McWhorter, I may have contributed to the antipathy underlying our contact. I no doubt was guilty of harboring a suspicious hatred of the nemesis so acutely hated by my father in my formative years, when he had instilled a kind of social virus in me in his diatribes against the *goyim*'.

That I became a more universalistic person later in life and overcame my background is likely a delayed benefit of my war adventures, which provided a corrective experience through social interchanges with the non-Jewish world. This helped me escape from the xenophobic psychological cocoon into which I was born. I had a notably positive living experience as a member of the *Myakin'* B-24 crew, where over many combat missions, we crewmen learned to depend upon each other and to work smoothly together in periods of danger. Though we were a diverse group, coming from nine different states, affectionate ties grew among us. The feeling of brotherhood pervading our first reunion after the war, some forty-five years after we had last seen each other, proved rewarding and made me realize how much I cared for these men.

Notes:

1. Joseph Heller, *Catch-22* (New York: Simon and Schuster, 1966), p. 211.

Pilot Jim McLain and the B-24 Liberator Myakin'

18

Christmas in Casablanca

December 16, 1944: Having just completed my assigned quota of combat missions, I was taking leave of the 450th Bomb Group and the air base outside of the town of Manduria in the heel of Italy that had been my home for the last six months.

I felt euphoric about having come through the air war in Europe with my body whole. Flying thirty-nine sorties over enemy territory without getting killed surely defined me as a lucky guy. I retained this point of view even though the scuttlebutt around the base was that I would be shipped out, after a rest furlough in the States, to participate in the air war against Japan.

In flying combat missions, it had been my practice that if I was not scheduled to fly on a given day, I would tell myself: *"You are alive today and that is all that counts."* I had thus managed to achieve a complete state of relaxation. At this moment, I was luxuriating in the heartening fact that I was going home, and looking forward to a reunion with my family and any of my old friends who happened to be available.

The only down side to my leaving Manduria was separating from my crew. In the course of my combat experience I had come to appreciate how closely together we ten men on McLain's crew had bonded. The shared experience of war had connected us in important ways, as if we were brothers. I wondered if I would ever see them again.

I visited the tarmac where the maintenance crew was working on our airplane, *Myakin'*. I affectionately patted the familiar figure painted on the nose section: a donkey kicking its hind legs high into the air. Over the time we had flown together, the plane itself had come symbolize the connections among us, identifying us as a crew.

After getting my travel papers at squadron headquarters and returning my flying paraphernalia to the supply officer, I bid my farewells and caught a military plane to Naples, officially becoming "an officer in transit." Returning home by air, I could avoid a long, dreary boat trip across the Atlantic, where attacks by German submarines were still a possibility.

My itinerary was many-legged, with overnight layovers at places I had never been before: first, to Casablanca in North Africa; then to Dakar on the west coast of Senegal; then across the Atlantic Ocean to Rio de Janeiro in Brazil; on to Puerto Rico; and finally to Miami. From Florida, I would journey home to New York City by train.

I took advantage of a two-day layover in Naples to visit Pompeii, Herculaneum, and other tourist sites. It felt good to be using my senses in the appreciation of artistic artifacts. Museum-hopping made me feel civilized, and certainly it was a gentler and more enjoyable pursuit than sweating out bombing raids on places like Budapest's railroad yards. But I was not exactly buoyant, since it felt lonely to be on my own for the first time since I had entered the service two years before.

I wondered what the guys were doing in Manduria as they faced their last missions. Was Caserta still writing passionate love letters to that girl back home he had never met? Was Jim McLain going to get that well-deserved promotion to the rank of captain? Was another crew being prepared to take over *Myakin'*? I thought warmly about how well our B-24 airplane served us over so many missions.

The next day, I arrived in Casablanca in the early afternoon, and the beauty of the city made me eager to taste the delights it might have to offer. After stowing my things at the transit officers' barracks, I took off to explore the modern area of the city. It struck me as being very French in appearance and cosmopolitan in the way public life was organized. Christmas decorations were displayed on the main streets, and save for the absence of snow, what I saw reminded me of the holiday atmosphere back home. People on the street appeared well dressed, particularly the women. The contrast with the drab attire of their counterparts in southern Italy, where formless black dresses were uniformly worn, was readily apparent. I also ventured into the Muslim quarters of the city, which though poor provided their own sources of visual stimulation.

With a few days of waiting before I went on to Dakar, I spent my time in aimless meandering around Casablanca, taking in the sights and listening to the novel sounds of foreign languages. The ambiance of the setting evoked exotic sensations in my brain.

A youngster about twelve years of age, apparently European, spotted me and started walking beside me. Speaking French, he attempted to engage me in conversation. Obviously fascinated by my American military uniform with navigator's wings displayed on my chest, he asked me if I had served in the war against the *Boche*. He expressed enthusiastic approval when I replied in the affirmative.

I inquired: *"Etes-vous français?"* His reply was sharply negative: *"Non! Je suis juif."* His strong affirmation of his Jewish identity impressed me. And it clearly pleased him when I responded, *"Moi aussi."*

My walking companion's name was Claude, and from what I could glean from our brief conversation, he and his parents had come to Casablanca as refugees from Nazi-occupied France. He told me there were many Jewish families in the city at this time. I offered him an American chocolate bar, and he ran off to rejoin friends waiting for him down the block.

This conversation with Claude allowed me to present myself in an encounter with a person outside the military as someone with a history of participation in the war, someone who took risks in an active combat role. To be able to identify myself this way felt singularly good, and I had to recognize a reservoir of boastfulness lurking within me. Of course this was not the image I wanted to project, because I knew millions of human beings had been risking their lives in this war. Yet, it felt good to be able to provide this Jewish youngster, whose family had had to flee Hitler's troops, an example of a Jew who was not a victim, one who participated in retaliatory actions against the enemy.

In examining my feelings, I recognized the irony in my situation, because this self-pride in being a Jew was not my normal state of mind. Rather, it was exactly the orientation of my father, Hyman Fanshel. His zeal about Jewishness was like a repeated drumbeat and was off-putting because he seemed prejudiced against our non-Jewish friends. But now at the end of my combat tour, when meeting a displaced child like Claude, his forceful advocacy seemed less misplaced.

By late afternoon, I was tired after several hours of walking the streets of the city. My mood had changed, and I was feeling dispirited, conscious again of the sense of social isolation in no longer being a part of a close-knit aircrew.

As much to get the load off my feet as to obtain liquid refreshment, I decided to find a watering hole on a local neighborhood street. After passing a few restaurants and bars, I entered a bistro called Jolie's Bar, very spacious and crowded with patrons. A number of waiters and waitresses were taking orders on the run under the strict oversight of the barrel-chested owner. Wearing a white half-apron, he was omnipresent and appeared to know almost everybody in the place.

I found a seat at a small table close to the door and ordered a glass of vermouth. A drinking crowd provided the main action, and I observed that the patrons were obviously using the late afternoon for convivial relief from the cares of the day. A pianist sang popular French songs while men and women surrounded the piano, drinks in hand. Seeming to ignore the music, they were engaged in animated discussion punctuated with outbreaks of hearty laughter. As the only American in the place, I envied the upbeat mood they displayed.

Taking in the ambience of the bar, I playfully scanned the scene before me. I pretended I was sitting in the nose turret of a B-24 on a combat mission. Using the navigational technique of dead reckoning, I found myself focusing upon a woman leaning on the piano chatting with a male companion. She was facing him, away from me, and all I saw was her back. My attention was engaged as she leaned forward, raising her shapely posterior and affording a pleasing view. A "target of opportunity," as we used to say on missions with the 450th. Interested, I spotted her in the cross-hairs of my psychic drift meter. As if I were on a bomb run over the Ploesti oil fields, I carefully tracked her body from the I.P. (initial point)—her head—down to the target—her behind. I sensed a stirring in my loins responsive to her evocative configuration. *Navigator to pilot: "Target straight ahead. Open the bomb bay doors!"*

As I stared at this "target" of visual opportunity, I was stimulated to remember a recreational performance presented at the 450th Bomb Group's open-air theater in Manduria. We were offered a demonstration of belly dancing provided by Zoria, the Egyptian Dancing Girl, by far the most popular program during my stay in Manduria.

We airmen lived with a great deal of stress, reflected in our almost compulsive talk about hairy moments in tough missions and concern about the odds of returning home whole. It clearly was essential for our mental health that recreational activity be provided to help us relax in body and mind, and the commander of the 450th saw that opportunities for amusement were provided. Distractions that could take our minds off the hazards we faced were made available on a frequent basis, and included programmatic activity such as sports contests, movies, and shows put on by visiting stars and theater groups.

Amusements that catered to the masculine interests of the men were particularly popular. Thus, much enthusiasm was shown when our base was visited by Joe Louis, the heavyweight boxing champion of the world. He came across as an amiable celebrity with interesting stories to tell about his boxing career, and we were impressed with his ability to share the experiences he had had in the ring.

Yet the single interest that most met a craving desire of the men was *women,* and the sexier the examples of the fair gender the better, and that, hands down, was Zoria, the Egyptian Dancing Girl.

The seating arrangements for the show were unusual. The U.S. Army Air Corps had the reputation of being one of the most democratic organizations participating in the war. After all, officers and enlisted men shared exposure to the same fate on the hazardous missions flown on the heavy bombers. If a plane blew up or got shot down, all the men on board, regardless of rank, were subject to the same fate.

However, the arrival of Zoria was a different situation, and exposed the prevailing class differences between ranks of officers and enlisted men. The avowal of the full expression of democracy in the ranks was clearly a sham. In the front row, seats were assigned in order to colonels, lieutenant colonels, and majors. Then rows of captains, followed by second lieutenants and flight officers. Then came the enlisted men, with master sergeants first and buck privates assigned to the "cheap seats" way in the rear. While all came with service-issued binoculars, it was clear that rank had its privileges.

Sophisticated scholars of Middle Eastern cultural customs have let it be known that belly dancing has a venerable tradition and is a quite respected dance form. It is not considered lowbrow when seen in its authentic cultural context. Nevertheless, when belly dancing takes place at an airfield where female companionship has been denied men for extended periods, the performance is apt to be viewed from a different perspective. In this instance, no artist has ever had a more attentive audience.

It was impressive, and almost frightening, to hear evidence of the responsiveness of gonads of hundreds of men to the sight of gyrating female flesh. The sound that swept across the audience started as a low hum, became something of a growl, and finally came forth in massive trombone-like sounds that suggested men in agony. As intended by the program planners, a truly uplifting cultural experience had been provided for the men of the 450th.

Absorbed in erotic ruminations, I had become psychologically detached from my location in Jolie's Bar. When I broke out of my trance, I saw the man talking to the woman who was the focus of my escape into libidinal fantasy suddenly lean forward and whisper into her ear. Straightening abruptly, she whirled her head around and caught me ogling her with the gaze of a forlorn lover. I was startled to realize that I had been exposed as a voyeur, and my cheeks began to burn under her censorious gaze. I considered a hasty retreat from the place. But then the woman's countenance relaxed and she broke into a laugh. Warming to her friendly smile, I became sufficiently at ease to share in the humor of the situation.

Now that this object of my fantasies had turned around, I observed that she was indeed attractive. About ten years older than I, she had brunette hair with a cut that left a teased curl dangling in the middle of her forehead. The structure of her face reminded me of Marlene Deitrich. She was draped in a close-fitting dress that reflected French styling, and her make-up was not restrained. To my eyes, she was a provocative beauty. I wondered whether her continued gaze in my direction was a sign that she was open to becoming involved with me.

I suspected my uniform had stimulated this female stranger's interest. Having medals and flight insignia on my chest may have made my image more dashing and cavalier. A bit more manly, shall we say? Unfortunately, I realized that my focus upon my attire was a cover for a sense of insecurity that lay below the surface of my presentation of myself as a worldly fellow. To my consternation, the inspection I was receiving made me shaky and unsure, more the inexperienced schoolboy than the man about town.

My heart skipped a beat when whoever-she-was began to walk toward me. She moved through the throng in a leisurely manner, with a graceful sway to her hips. The waiter seemed to know her and, responding to her gesture, made a chair available next to me. In introducing herself, she leaned forward and our proximity introduced an air of intimacy between us. She spoke in a soft, melodious tone, and I was calmed by her gentle laughter. She communicated in a hybrid of English and French, and I responded in my primitive high school French.

I soon learned that my newfound companion's name was Marianne. She mentioned that she had arrived in Casablanca a few years ago from a town near Marseilles. She had no family with her, and it was not clear how she supported herself.

Marianne showed interest in me and asked probing questions that focused upon military life and the perks that went with being an officer. She explored specific areas, such as the pay and allowances we received, and the nature of our living quarters and recreational activities. She nodded approvingly when she learned that I had been assigned a small private room at the transit officers' quarters. "Very convenient," she said with a suggestive smile.

Because of the nature of Marianne's questions, I suspected that she might have had an enemy intelligence connection, and I resolved to be cautious in what I said. We had been warned in security briefings that the Germans deployed attractive women in the hope of extracting military information from gullible GI's. Or was I just getting paranoid?

We wound up in Marianne's apartment near the bistro. The transfer to her residence was negotiated simply. "David, it is too noisy to talk here. Would you like to come to my place for a drink?" I understood that a sexual encounter was in the offing. Why else would she invite me to her apartment? After all of the prewar years of obsessive talk about sex, in the locker room at Schiff Center where I participated in sports, the time for launching my adult life was at hand. I was thankful I was not dealing with one of those "cock-teasers" from the Grand Concourse, because these on-again, off-again middle-class Jewish girls used to drive us guys out of our minds. But I was also aware that my heart was pumping away, and I was coping with a low-grade sense of fear. I overcame such signs of cowardice with self-reassuring reflections on the fact that, after flying scary missions through flak-strewn clouds over major German targets, this was going to be a "milk run." I no longer had to prove myself to anyone.

Marianne's place of residence was a somewhat ancient and grimy-looking four-story building situated in a working-class district. Her top-floor apartment was quite small and modest in its furnishings. There was a main room that served simultaneously as a kitchen, dining area, and bedroom. The pieces of furniture included her double bed, a large and ornate armoire, a wooden chest of drawers, and a small dining table with two chairs. Two shaded lamps placed upon decorative iron stands provided muted lighting. The overhead light was turned off, helping to create a romantic atmosphere. On her bed was a scattering of well-dressed dolls, giving a feminine ambience to the room. There was also an attached closet-sized room with a toilet and a sink.

Marianne closed the entrance door to her apartment, secured the lock, and turned to me with a welcoming kiss upon my cheek. The strong fragrance of her perfume was very pleasing in its effect. Something significant was transpiring between us, and I was turned on. No doubt about it, my senses were on the alert and my attention was focused. I readily accepted the offer of a glass of brandy in the hope that it might calm me down.

Marianne put a musical record on her wind-up record player and opened her arms for me to dance with her. The mournful female voice I heard sounded like Edith Piaf singing one of her cabaret songs about a tragic love affair. I managed to move Marianne around the limited space of the room in my standard ungainly version of the two-step, and her eyes seemed to be gently laughing at me. She felt soft and feminine in my arms, and I was floating on a cloud.

When the record stopped, Marianne opened a subject with which she seemed preoccupied. At first, I did not comprehend what she was saying, and I had a sense that our bilingual communication was breaking down. When she repeated herself, talking at a slower pace, her message became clear. She was proposing that I move in with her for the rest of my stay in Casablanca on condition that she be allowed to take advantage of dining privileges at the transit officers' dining hall. It seemed obvious that she had had prior experience with this kind of an arrangement, and that our relationship was going to be a quid pro quo affair.

Caught by surprise, I asked myself what this was all about. Clearly, I was unprepared to respond to her offer. I wondered whether I was stepping into a misadventure, one that I would come to regret. This was definitely not going to be a hit-and-run proposition.

To ease the atmosphere, Marianne offered me some candy. She opened her armoire and exposed a remarkable sight. I saw before me about fifty neatly stacked cans of Whitman's chocolates. I also noticed an assemblage of tins of smoked oysters; artichoke hearts; packages of dried mushrooms; cans of coffee, sardines, and anchovies; bottles of Cognac; and other fancy delicacies—items one would expect to find in an expensive gourmet shop.

I was particularly fascinated with Marianne's cache of Whitman's chocolates. The item was only occasionally available at our post exchange, and when shipments came in they were quickly sold out. Once, when our plane was damaged by flak and it became necessary to land at an airfield near Ancona, in the north of Italy, our main concern was to inform group headquarters by radio that we had not been shot down. We demanded that steps be taken to protect our belongings from our foraging comrades in the barracks. I was particularly concerned that nobody filch my precious can of Whitman's chocolates, secretly stashed away among my personal belongings.

The armoire's bounteous contents suggested to me that there had been a parade of men going through Marianne's apartment. In fact, I felt sure she had cast a wide net in making available her sexual charms to American servicemen, and perhaps to others. While I could sympathize with her survival needs in wartime, food being in scarce supply, I was obviously not prepared to take on the role of a social missionary!

I realized that I had been very naive and should have known immediately that I was in the apartment of a prostitute. I was not prepared to be a bold john-seeking-to-get-laid on a pay-as-you-go basis. I was influenced in my attitude by my recall of films seen in basic training that dealt with the consequences of contracting venereal disease. The grisly film images of the desiccated penises of luckless GI's were called up from memory. They were selected by the Medical Corps to impact upon our psyches and had been very effective in repressing any impulse to consort with women who might be picked up in the streets near military bases. Their viewing even killed sexy dreams for awhile.

I decided that after surviving a tour of combat on a B-24 with my body quite intact, it would be foolish to allow myself to be "shot down" in a passing fling in Casablanca. Marianne's offer was very tempting, but it would be poor form for the would-be hero to return to the warm embrace of his family with a raging case of syphilis or the "clap."

My combat experience had prepared me to take precipitous action, and I quickly resolved my dilemma. I beat a hasty retreat, mumbling the fiction that I was a married man with a young wife and infant child at home. I just could not turn my back on my obligations. With a look of astonishment, Marianne stared at me silently. She was nonplussed. She clearly had not met my type before. I saw a pained look on her face, and I wondered if prostitutes were personally hurt when prospective customers turn them down. Did they feel rejected, as if their personal attributes did not measure up to some standard? That they were not beautiful enough? Despite a pang of conscience, my instincts for self-preservation remained operative, and I unlatched the door and dashed down the stairs and into the street.

On the way back to the transit officers' quarters I kept muttering:

"Damn!

"Damn!

"Goddamn!

"Twenty-one years old and still a virgin!"

The Author with His Sister Ruth, January 1945

19

Two Flyboys Home from the Air War

In January 1945, I arrived home for a long-awaited rest leave and recovery. Having flown in stages from Italy to Florida, I had taken an overnight train to New York City, reaching my family's apartment house in the Bronx at 7 A.M. My coming awakened my parents, who opened the apartment door to greet me in their sleeping wear. They appeared older and more worn looking than when I had seen them more than a year before, an impression due in some part to their not having inserted their dentures prior to answering the door.

Copious tears flowed from my parents' eyes as they gave thanks to God that I had come home safely. It took an exceptional effort to refrain from joining them in the tearful display.

Over the next few days, my parents and I seemed to talk endlessly about my experiences in the war. I was able to catch up with my family's activities and adjust to the fact that both of my brothers were married, and that Sol and his wife, Florence, were parents of a young child, Susan. My sister, Ruth, enlivened by her engagement to Wallace Berger, was avidly looking forward to his return from the war. A homecoming party was arranged on a Sunday, with our large extended family crowding into the small two-bedroom Bronx apartment. It reminded me of a similar occasion when I turned thirteen, and my bar mitzvah was celebrated with a family gathering of about fifty people in our home.

A short time later, another reunion took place, when I had the opportunity to spend some time with Rocky (fictitious name), a good friend from the prewar years. I knew Rocky as a fellow member of a boy's athletic club, the Lions. We played basketball in the gymnasium at the Jacob H. Schiff Center, the Jewish community center at Fordham Road and Valentine Avenue in the Bronx.

We members of the Lions owned green athletic jackets with the club name emblazoned on the back. The jackets and basketball uniforms gave us prestige and were worn with youthful exuberance. There was no connection between our affiliation with the sports program at the Center and the religious orientations of our parents. Our interest was exclusively focused on sports, and you didn't have to be Jewish to belong. One of our members was Billy Reilly, an Irish-American friend.

Apart from our absorption with sports, we hung out at Poe Park, located on the Grand Concourse, the middle-class residential area in the northern section of the Bronx later featured in Paddy Chayefsky's TV drama and film *Marty*. Although we were younger, our social group closely resembled the one portrayed in the film. In addition to sports, the usual topic of conversation that occupied us was sex. As teenagers midway in our high-school careers, we were responding to glandular urgings with an avid interest in girls as physical objects for study and analysis. It seems we never tired of talking about the subject.

When the United States entered the war, our group averaged about eighteen years of age, and we expected that we would be drafted into the military before long. Seeking to have some choice in the matter, Rocky, like me, volunteered for service in the Army Air Corps, while other Lions members enlisted in the tank corps, parachutist service, infantry, and navy. Our young ages and romantic notions about the heroic roles we would be called upon to perform displaced any thought that we would be maimed or killed while participating in hazardous ventures against the Nazis. Our orientation was in the here and now, and danger was not perceived as imminent. (Several years later, with the realities of conflict fully experienced, wisdom took hold and there was not a trace of the notion that participating in warfare had provided uplifting personal benefits for us.)

When I came home from Italy in early January 1945, Rocky also returned, but as I learned through various mutual friends, Rocky's story was different from mine. I had come home intact. Although I was described by those close to me as quite tense and somewhat grim, I was otherwise in good physical shape. Whatever emotional residue remained from the flights over Ploesti, Munich, and Vienna would dissipate over time. But this was not true of Rocky's situation.

Rocky had seen considerable action in combat. He had become a flight engineer and gunner on a B-17 Flying Fortress assigned to the 8th Air Force flying out of England. Most of the missions on which he flew took him deep into German territory and involved heavily defended targets. Rocky and his crewmates had participated in frequent air battles with the Luftwaffe and usually encountered fearful antiaircraft artillery fire. He was flying somewhat earlier in the war than myself, and his chances for survival were more dismal than mine, close to zero for a predetermined combat tour of thirty-five missions.

The inevitable happened one day when Rocky's aircraft took a direct hit in the bomb bay. The plane plummeted from the sky, resembling a burning meteor. Miraculously, Rocky was able to extricate himself from the falling plane before it crashed. In the split seconds available to him, he managed to pull his parachute cord, and he landed safely on German soil.

Rocky's survival came at a cost so severe that instant death might have been a kinder outcome. His face and other parts of his body were so severely burned by the fire engulfing his plane that his appearance as he lay on the ground was that of a destroyed animal, one that had been ravaged by a more powerful predator. His face had been transformed into a moon-like spherical object, and gashes, ridges, and gullies scored the glistening skin of his face. One could imagine that he had been washed over by the hot lava of an explosive volcano. Particularly affecting upon the viewer was the fact that there were no apertures to serve as recognizable markers of a human countenance. His scalp had been burned off, and his eyes were sealed shut. His nose and ears were gone, and his mouth was welded tight.

Whatever the horror of Rocky's condition as he lay on the ground, he was still alive. The German military men who found his prostrate body felt some compassion for him. A sense of common humanity prevailed despite the fact that the fallen airman was a participant in the bombing assaults that were wreaking destruction upon many German cities and were killing and maiming tens of thousands of residents. Rocky's captors organized emergency medical care for the burnt flier, and surgeons worked on necessary life-saving tasks that included the opening of his eyelids and mouth. Most important, they administered painkillers that reduced the intolerable sensate war raging within his body.

At the stalag prisoner-of-war camp in Germany, where he stayed for many months, Rocky was given little treatment beyond what was required to sustain his life. There was no cosmetic surgery administered, so he had to daily face the reality that his face was a harsh witness to the brutality of war. He was frightening to look at, especially to himself.

A change in Rocky's life came when the International Red Cross arranged for the exchange of very disabled prisoners between Germany and the United States. Rocky was sent home in the fall of 1944 and was hospitalized at Valley Forge Hospital near Philadelphia, where severely disfigured personnel were being treated. When I had my first meeting with him, he had received about fifteen surgical operations whose purpose was to reconstruct his face. Over the coming years, he was to undergo many more operations. It was necessary to rebuild his facial features, including his nose, lips, eyelids, and eyebrows. Luckily, there were parts of his body that had not been burned, and some areas could be used for the materials that could reconstitute his face. His eyebrows had been created from the hair behind his neck. His nose had been reconstructed, and patches of skin from his back were used to provide new areas of facial normalcy. But in looking at him, one saw a patchwork quilt made of skin that was blotched, uneven in surface texture, and very discolored

Still on recreational leave from the Air Corps, I learned that Rocky was on a break from the hospital, recuperating from the latest operation to reconstruct his face. When I contacted him, he agreed to come with me to Sea Gate to visit with my parents, who had rented an apartment in this seaside resort community in Brooklyn adjacent to Coney Island. We hoped to enjoy walking along the beach and going on the carnival rides at Luna Park.

I made an appointment to rendezvous with Rocky in Times Square, where we could take the subway to Brooklyn. As the time approached for me to go into Manhattan to meet him, I sensed that I was uneasy as I contemplated our first encounter. I found myself remembering Rocky as a fellow member of our sports club the year before we entered military service. He was then a handsome, masculine youth, with lush black hair combed straight back, even features, and a spectacular body build. He had the combined attributes we later associated with a Sylvester Stallone and a youthful Charles Bronson. Although he was somewhat full of himself, the way good-looking adolescents can be, the girls found him irresistible. After a post-game shower, he would stand in front of the mirror in the locker room and carefully comb his hair and stare at his own image. I was not sure how I would react in viewing the evidence of burn damage all over his face.

When I arrived at our meeting place, I spotted a young man in uniform looking around at the people passing by, and his eyes came to rest on me. He smiled and nodded his head emphatically. I surmised the person coming forward to connect with me was Rocky.

A welter of reactions swept over me. Rocky was not, of course, immediately recognizable, because he bore no resemblance to my boyhood friend. Although well worked over by the plastic surgeons, his physical reconstruction was still a work in progress, and he was a shocking apparition even to strangers encountering him on the street. Although I had previously seen burn victims at a military hospital in Italy, I was not prepared for this first encounter with Rocky. The overall effect was too painful to absorb. *"So this is what happens when your plane blows up!"*

A strained silence ensued as Rocky looked steadily at me. He appeared to be testing the waters to determine whether I was up to facing what he had been through. I struggled to find appropriate words of greeting. Finally, I simply said nothing and grabbed him in a bear hug. Our embrace broke the barrier between us, and we quickly fell into the familiar talk of flyboys who have seen action on heavy bombers.

We took the subway to my parents' vacation place in Sea Gate. My father was away taking care of some business in Manhattan, and my mother had a friend visiting her. Although I had prepared her for the visit, Mom turned ghostly white when she saw Rocky for the first time. She stared for a moment and then recovered. She knew he was one of my chums from Schiff Center, but his marred appearance prevented her from recognizing him. She appeared even more distressed than I was at our first encounter and was in danger of bursting into tears. But she mobilized herself sufficiently to offer us cookies and ice cream, and managed to engage us in small talk. But the meaning of Rocky's plight seemed to penetrate her very being.

I found myself acutely aware of my mother's thought processes. She had recently told me that it had been psychological torture for her to know that I was flying over German-controlled Europe in an airplane loaded with bombs and in danger of being shot down. While overseas, I had written home from Italy, keeping score for my parents on the missions I had completed, with the expectation of returning home after the fiftieth. The waiting had been hell for her. In a life full of tragic events, the death of a young child in transit to the United States among them, Clara had developed a capacity to imagine every conceivable misfortune that could happen to her children. We knew her to be nervous about us in all sorts of ways. For example, prior to the departure of the three of us for the military, it was common for her to hang out of the window of our apartment at late hours in midwinter, straining to catch a glimpse of us coming home after an evening's recreation. Rocky represented for her the disaster that had been avoided in our family, and she was acutely aware of the heartbreak he represented for his mother and father.

Rocky and I had a carefree time at the beach and then headed for the amusement park at Coney Island, where we enjoyed going on all the available rides. We stuffed ourselves with hot dogs, cotton candy, and candied apples and washed everything down with soda pop. When evening approached, we took the subway into Manhattan and headed for the nightclubs on 52nd Street. We heard great jazz performers, including renderings of the late Fats Waller's "My Feet's Too Big," and we were joined by other servicemen on leave. As they became aware of Rocky's condition, the reactions of civilian patrons at the bars and restaurants were telling. Women revealed a particular intensity, with expressions of disbelief and emotional distress similar to the reaction shown by my mother.

A heartwarming feature of Rocky's story was that his long-time girlfriend, Matilda (fictitious name), remained committed to their relationship after his return, and there were plans for them to marry. In many ways, she was admired by Rocky's old friends for her personal fortitude and values. She was regarded as almost as intrepid as he was in the journey she was prepared to travel. It was very common for youthful commitments to marriage, such as had been made by Rocky and Matilda, to be cast aside after the war. This took place because of the profound alterations in the outlooks and understandings of each of the pair. Matilda had compelling reasons to change her mind: Her handsome prince was no longer the man he had been before the war, on the outside at least. But she held fast to her commitment, and the marriage proved long lasting. Together, they built a family resembling those of the other members of the Lions, myself included.

In his own right, Rocky reflected an extraordinary fortitude that enabled him to rise above his misfortune. Early on in his recovery, he displayed the same cockiness that was a core personality characteristic of his adolescent years, when he had played football, hockey, and basketball in a very aggressive style. On the day of our first encounter in the spring of 1945, when we had a date to "do the town," it was clear to me that he had no intention of sparing others the discomfort of having to look at his destroyed visage. Every day provided chance encounters with strangers, or with old friends and acquaintances, who had to absorb meeting Rocky's most compelling attribute: his disfigurement. His body language and way of conducting himself gave a clear communication in confronting the unprepared observer: *"This is what war does. If you can't face it, tough shit!"*

Ferrara Railroad Bridge Bomb Strike Photo, a Site of the Accelerated Po Valley River Battle

20

Epilogue: The Ultimate Absurdity

What had happened to Rocky provided me with a reality check about the acts of warfare in which I had recently participated. His burned face was forever etched upon my brain, and it symbolized in my mind one of the major destructive forces unleashed by the weaponry of contemporary warfare: severe burn injuries bringing disfigurement and death. As the years have passed, the fate of the human beings who had resided in close proximity to our bombing targets continued to loom large in my consciousness.

Friends and family members occasionally have asked me if I felt guilty about having engaged in actions in which bombs were rained upon helpless civilians. I find no easy answers to such questions. True, we were striking at factories, not usually at people, but our aim was not always accurate, and there must have been quite a number of human casualties because of our actions. I thus belatedly confront the ethical issues faced by combatants when following orders from the military command. What responsibility did we carry in inflicting misery on men, women, and children who were not involved in the fighting?

I invariably respond that we were involved in no-holds-barred warfare on both sides, and the outcome of this worldwide armed conflict depended upon whoever could mobilize the most destructive force against the opponent. For us, a victory by the Nazi military was unthinkable.

I do not remember much discussion about the victimization of civilians among airmen. The closest we came in Manduria to discussing such an issue was the acute concern about possibly having to bail out of a disabled plane. It would be stressful, to say the least, to find oneself parachuting amidst the local population who had experienced the horror of our actions while we flew over them. There had been frequent reports about the lynching of downed airmen by outraged German citizens.

Truth to tell, when we dropped bombs on factories from an altitude of twenty thousand feet or more and happened to hit the people working in them, we were spared having to confront the havoc we had unleashed. We could breathe a sigh of relief when we heard the announcement over the intercom, "Bombs away," and desired nothing more than to have those words followed by the pilot declaiming: "Let's get the hell out of here!"

Over the years, however, I have had opportunities to meet individuals who experienced some of these same events from a very different perspective. One of the first was an encounter with a fellow student while I was attending Columbia University in 1950.

My wife and I were living in a small apartment on 106th Street near Riverside Drive in Manhattan, about ten blocks south of Columbia University. The proximity of the university encouraged me to act on the idea I had been toying with of studying for an advanced degree in sociology. I chose to test the waters by enrolling in a graduate course with the famed professor Robert K. Merton, one of the country's most distinguished sociologists.

I was able to enroll in Columbia's doctoral program free of personal cost through the GI Bill of Rights. Before doing so, however, I was required to undergo tests and interviews by the

Veterans Administration staff to determine whether extending my educational benefits would be a valid use of further federal support. Since I had already completed a master's degree program in social work, they wanted to know if my interest in sociology was indicative of an uncertainty about my career objectives. Simply put: Was this former air warrior simply flitting around because education is available as a veteran's free benefit?

After elaborate testing, in a conference with an advisor I was told that the results "clearly indicate that you should be a social worker or a sociologist." I thought: *"At last! There is order in the universe."*

The class with Merton was exhilarating, and he proved to be an extraordinary lecturer whose reputation was well deserved. It was as if each word had been sandpapered and polished.

One day, I was sitting next to an attractive, well-dressed woman about my age, and it wasn't long before I found out that she was a foreign student of Italian background residing in the United States for a year to enhance her education. Her English was quite good.

I spontaneously revealed that I had a significant sojourn with the U.S. military stationed in the heel of Italy, the Puglia region. When she inquired about my experiences there, I told her about our bombing trips on B-24's to destroy German targets.

Changing the subject, because I realized that people who had lived through the war in Europe may not wish to engage in idle conversation about it, I attempted an innocent inquiry:

"And what part of Italy do you come from, may I ask?"

My fellow student, Sophia by name, responded with some pride. "I come from an old city on the Po River that most Americans manage to skip by when touring my country. Ferrara is a beautiful place with lovely city walls containing walkways on top; it is south of Venice and Padua and important in the history of Italy."

My interest was aroused by the mention of Ferrara and, despite my resolve not to talk about the war, I found myself revealing an important fact of my history: "That's a coincidence. I flew over Ferrara twice in the summer of 1944, a mere six years ago. I was on an American bomber plane and we were attempting to destroy the big bridge on the Po River to prevent German troops from gaining support in men and supplies in the fierce conflict that was going on. As I remember it, we really clobbered the bridge."

Upon hearing this information, Sophia stiffened and stared intensely at me for awhile. Finally she blurted out: "You guys were a bunch of miserable, stupid asses! Bombing civilian populations as recklessly as you did is nothing to be proud of."

I realized that I had stepped into a minefield and began back-peddling desperately. I meekly replied: "It is true, once we dropped our bombs we could create unintended damage to innocent people, especially if we missed our targets. Were you personally affected by the American bombing raids?"

Sophia thrust her face close to mine and sarcastically launched a tirade: " 'Personally affected,' you ask? You Americans have a way of absolving yourselves of all kinds of cruelty because you think your intentions are the highest. Yes, I and my family were 'personally affected' by your 'unintended consequences.' You bombed our family's farm and home right near the bridge. You shattered our living quarters, killed our animals, and made the land impossible to farm for a long time. With your kind of help, you inflicted more direct harm on us than the Nazis did."

Completing her explosive outpouring, Sophia tossed her head in a dismissive gesture and marched off in a huff. Chastened by her sense of outrage, I could imagine the pain we had caused. I resolved to stop talking about the war to strangers.

I attended Professor Merton's class the following week. Although I expected cool disdain after Sophia's verbal assault in our previous encounter, I was relieved when she approached me with a smile and insisted upon apologizing for having been so wrathful. She shook my hand and assured me that the liberation of Italy from the fascist and Nazi yoke by American soldiers was still very much appreciated by her family. Removed from purgatory, I was pleased when Sophia accepted an invitation to have dinner with Florence and me at our home.

Epilogue: The Ultimate Absurdity

Upon reflection, I found Sophia's report on the destructive features of our military intervention in her country sobering. Though our actions were well intended, it did not spare noncombatants from a horrendous experience.

By contrast, many years later I had another encounter with an individual who had witnessed the bombing raids in which I had taken part. It was 1993, and my wife and I were invited as dinner guests to the home of friends who also lived in Teaneck, New Jersey, a town in which we had resided for about thirty-five years. We had met our hosts, Dijon and Marta Gruenberger, in Rome in 1968 when I was on a semester's sabbatical from Columbia University.

The Gruenbergers were a remarkable couple who had survived the Holocaust experienced by Jews in Czechoslovakia. Marta endured a spell in Auschwitz, where she befriended Dijon's sister, and this was how our friends had met and decided to marry. Dijon had escaped from the forced labor camp where he was being held, and had survived and rebuilt his life so well that after the war he became a major figure in biogenetic research in Prague and later in the United States. He also became a major contributor to cancer research at Columbia University, and the Gruenberger sons became well-established physicians.

There were other guests present who, like their hosts, were survivors of the Holocaust. In the course of the evening I talked with a man a few years older than myself and learned that he had been born and raised in Budapest. He asked if I had ever visited the city of his birth, and said that, despite his unhappy experiences, he still felt Budapest was a beautiful city. In a jocular manner, I informed him that I had the dubious pleasure of visiting Budapest three times in the summer of 1944, but not at the ground level. I explained that I had been a navigator on an American bomber flying at high altitudes over the city. On one occasion, we had bombed a bridge connecting Buda and Pest, and on another we had wreaked havoc with the city's railroad marshalling yards. We also had bombed an armaments factory, the Manfried Weiss Armament Works.

The man suddenly became ashen, staring intensely at me. With seeming great effort, he managed to collect his thoughts and tell me, "You will find this difficult to believe, but when you were bombing this factory, I was among the imprisoned Jewish laborers on the grounds of this industrial complex forced to turn out weapons to be used by the Germans against the Allies. We were in the ridiculous position of helping to provide murderers with weapons to be used against those who might save us. We prisoners were fixated on the armada of American planes glistening in the sky, and we chose not to seek shelter from the bombs coming down upon us. Our guards had abandoned us and retreated to shelters deep in the ground. We raised our arms shouting in our Czech language: 'Drop the bombs! Smash this place! Kill the bastards!'"

I was moved to learn that this man, a Holocaust survivor, and I were deeply connected by an event that had taken place so long ago.

Given these experiences, and from the vantage point of my senior years, I inquire of myself: Do my misgivings about burned civilians, evoked by the image of Rocky and the recognition of unintended consequences, such as those revealed by Sophia, signify that I would now oppose our bombing raids? My answer is in the negative.

On a personal level, my meeting with the Holocaust survivor who bore witness to the bombing of the Manfried Weiss Armament Works created for me a connection that brought out an identification with the millions of Jews that had been victimized by the Nazis. From a broader understanding, given the use of aerial warfare engaged in by the fascists in Spain and over western Europe, including the unrelenting bombing of London, aerial warfare had become an indispensable ingredient of military victory. The strategic bombing of German war assets, such as aircraft manufacturing factories, gasoline production facilities, and railroad marshalling yards, was an absolute requirement for Allied victory.

However, while I view the anti-Nazi struggle as having been inescapable, I would despair for the human race if we ever had to repeat the experience of such a worldwide catastrophe again. A motive in writing these memoirs is to put on record one more piece of individual testimony to join the multitudes who have expressed such concern: *World War II must be remembered for its unprecedented destructiveness. The human species would not survive another such experience.*

It was earnestly hoped that World War II would be the last war. But then came the Korean War, the Vietnam War, the Gulf War, Bosnia and Kosovo, Iraq, and now Afghanistan. The repeatedly shown inability to avoid war has become the ultimate absurdity.

Acknowledgements

I am grateful to my son, Ethan Fanshel, and daughter, Merrie (Fanshel) Jaffe, and her husband, Seth Jaffe, who have provided unfailing support in the years of my status as a single person. My five grandchildren have been a source of pleasure and have always lifted my spirits.

I thank Mariana Steinberg and my many friends, old and new, for continued sociability and shared pleasures.

I would like to acknowledge my fellow crew members on the *Myakin'* and others of the 450th Bomb Group. I am especially indebted to Jim McLain who, in later years, shared with me his notes on the missions we flew together, and to the 450th Website for their support of this project.

Special thanks are extended to Maria (Kookie) Plurad for her able nursing care at the Redwoods Retirement Center. She generously extended her ministrations to my computer when it would break down, and showed remarkable skill in both diagnosis and treatment. Bless her heart!

Barbara S. Brauer has been a Rock of Gibraltar in her professional service as my editor. She has unfailingly given me the space to formulate my own content of what information is required by the reader but will point to opportunities for my expansion of texts to meet the needs of the uninformed. She is masterly in the organization of text and has helped me stay on course.

Laurence Brauer has skillfully carried the stewardship of the photographs I have brought to this project. He has also garnered local New York City film shots of sites discussed in the book. His contribution has been helpful.

This book is intended for adults only. Parental guidance suggested.

Published Books by David Fanshel

B. Kutner, D. Fanshel, A. Togo, & T. Langner, *Five Hundred Over Sixty.* (New York: Russell Sage Foundation, 1956).

E. F. Borgatta, D. Fanshel, & H. Meyer, *Social Workers' Perceptions of Clients,* (New York: Russell Sage Foundation, 1960).

D. Fanshel, *Foster Parenthood,* (Minneapolis, Minn: University of Minnesota Press, 1960).

B. Jaffe, B. & D. Fanshel, *How They Fared in Adoption,* (New York: Columbia University Press, 1970).

D. Fanshel, & F. Moss, *Playback; a Marriage in Jeopardy Examined,* (New York: Columbia University Press, 1971).

D. Fanshel, *Far From the Reservation: The Transracial Adoption of American Indian Children,* (Metuchen, NJ: Scarecrow Press, 1972).

W. Labov, & D. Fanshel, *Therapeutic Discourse: Psychotherapy as Conversation.* New York: Academic Press, 1977).

D. Fanshel, & E. H Shinn, *Children in Foster Care: A Longitudinal Investigation,* (New York: Columbia University Press, 1978).

D. Fanshel, S. J. Finch, & J. F. Grundy, *Foster Children in a Life Course Perspective,* (New York: Columbia University Press, 1990).

D. Fanshel, S. J. Finch, & J. F. Grundy, *Serving the Urban Poor,* (New York: Praeger, 1992).

About the Author

David Fanshel was born in New York City in 1923, third of four children of immigrant Russian Jewish parents. As a teenager in the midst of the Depression, David watched his father struggle to support his family as a fruit wholesaler. When tragedy struck in 1936, the support of a network of extended relatives saved the family from disaster, but could not spare them from the stresses of their circumstances, which had significant ramifications for the younger generation.

A freshman at the City College of New York when war was declared in December 1941, David enlisted in the U.S. Army Air Corps, and served three years active duty from 1943 until 1945. He was commissioned as a navigator and flew 39 missions with the 15th Air Force 450th Bomb Group, 722nd Squadron, in Manduria, Italy. His targets included Ploesti, Vienna, Munich, Budapest, Toulon, and Athens. The only Jewish member in an air crew of ten men, the shared experiences in meeting the demands of combat had a transforming influence upon him and helped to overcome a xenophobic view of "goyim" brought by his immigrant family from oppressive experiences in pogrom-ridden czarist Russia.

After the war, Fanshel received his Masters Degree from the New York School of Social Work and a Doctorate at the Columbia University School of Social Work. His research career began as an associate in 1952 at Cornell University Medical College. In 1961 he joined the faculty at Columbia University School of Social Work and was a professor there until his retirement in 1993. In 1987, he was awarded a Secretary's Commemorative Award from the Department of Health and Human Services in the administration of President Ronald Reagan for his many research studies of vulnerable children.